They Used to Call Me Brother

A Memoir

Thomas H. Brennan

ISBN 978-1-7367887-0-7

"I am writing this book to please myself. It likely may not, and I have no idea whether it will please anyone else. The point is I want to clarify something in my own mind."

James Truslow Adams, *The American*, 1944

"The unexamined life is not worth living."

Socrates, Apology 38

Chapter 1

On a late spring evening in 1955, after all of the kids hurried home for supper, I hung around the school playground pretending to be busy until I gathered together my courage. I adjusted the web straps of my baseball glove, hoping none of my friends lingered and would see me.

Just before five I darted across the street, through a wrought iron gate, and onto the porch of a former convent where six Christian Brothers lived. The double doors, twice my height, loomed above me, but I concentrated on reciting the words I had memorized, "I think I have a religious vocation."

I pushed the doorbell. Nothing happened. I peered through the translucent glass but the heavy curtains inside blocked my view. At that moment I had two choices: abruptly abandon my plans and hurry home or remain steadfast. I chose the latter and rang the doorbell again. My perseverance changed my life.

Soon I heard footsteps and saw a dim light

shining through the curtains. Brother George, the principal of St. John's School, opened the door. I asked to see Brother Eugene, my eighth grade teacher. Brother George invited me in and led me into a formal parlor.

"Sit down," he said. "Brother Eugene will be right with you."

This parlor, unlike my apartment parlor, was posh: dark oak wainscoting and a massive portrait of St. John Baptist de la Salle, the founder of the Christian Brothers, dominating one wall. In the foyer, a chandelier hung over a carved wooden staircase leading to the second floor.

I sat on a Victorian couch; my feet on a thick carpet, my fingers fidgeting my baseball glove and gazed up at the tin ceiling atop twelve foot walls. Across the hallway I watched a votive light twinkling in the dark chapel.

Brother Eugene, a lanky man with a stretched neck, sunken cheeks and beady eyes on a face that tapered into a pointed crown on the back of his head entered the parlor. He wasn't wearing his black religious habit, only a pair of black pants and a white t-shirt.

I stood and blurted out, "I think I have a religious vocation." I have always been the type of person to get directly to the issue.

He answered, "Well, I think you should pray about it." I thought he would say, "Yes, you do," or "No, you don't." I figured the brothers had insight into these spiritual matters. Very few boys had a religious vocation. Only the holiest or those with the potential received a calling. Michael McVey, who sat behind me in Brother Eugene's class, copied every answer from my arithmetic tests. Certainly, a cheat like he would not be called.

Since I hadn't heard any voices nor had any dreams I only hinted that I possessed a vocation. I thought I had a vocation like I had the chickenpox; I had it but didn't know how I got it.

Brother Eugene calmed me. "If you think you're being called but you're not sure," he advised, "the best thing you can do is attend daily mass and pray more often." He escorted me into the candlelit chapel where I knelt in a pew, blessed myself and recited a short prayer. Nothing more than that; Brother Eugene exerted no pressure.

Even though I would only turn fourteen that summer of '55, I believed that evening I chose my life's path, to accept a call to the religious life. Sixteen years later I reexamined my motives, and realized one of the reasons I joined the Christian Brothers was to get away from my mother.

ॐॐ

Although I was only two, I remember vividly the pain.

My mother kept a baby book, one typical of the 1940s era, ten inches wide, eight inches high, an ivory satin cover embroidered with flowers and the title "Baby's Own Book." She noted many details that have enabled me to experience the pains and joys of my early childhood. Her extensive observations enabled me to recreate scenes in my infancy, and she continued writing comments until I had reached my teenage years.

In one section, entitled "Baby's Mental Development," my mother made an entry on November 1, 1943 when I was two under the heading entitled "Obedience." Her remark would be prophetic. My mother cherished the virtue of obedience and I evidently lacked it. "Tommy minds his Daddy very well. He does not always pay attention to his Mommy. Possibly because she is with him so much and Daddy sees him only at times." The last entry—also dated November 1, 1943—on the bottom of the same page in the section entitled "Response to punishment" triggered by memories. My mother wrote that Tommy "does not like to be spanked. Runs in bedroom, closes door and puts his head on bed and cries. Says 'Poor Tommy.'"

I have no recollection of my unruly behavior on that day when I was two years old. Whatever I did landed me firmly in the mortal, not venial, sin category, but even the sacrament of confession would not have spared me. My mother, exasperated by my antics, uttered the fateful words, "Just wait until your father comes home." I was young, but old enough to understand what would happen.

The sentence sounded like a promise but my mother voiced it as a threat. I picked up my toys hoping that my obedient behavior would assuage my mother's irritation and mitigate the punishment. Nevertheless, the inevitable had been put into motion. When my father came home from his job of driving a bus, he followed his usual custom—removed his motorman's hat, turned it upside down on the foyer bureau next to the black rotary dial telephone, emptied his pockets of loose change, handkerchief, key ring, wallet and removed his belt from his pants. He dumped everything inside the hat then curled the belt and set it inside the hat around the rim. He looked in the mirror over the bureau and ran his fingers through his thinning black hair.

On the evenings when the punishment would be meted out my mother and father held a quick conference about my misbehavior in which the details would be explained and my father, instead of coiling the belt in his cap, would wrap the belt around his left fist and come searching for me. It would be his duty to punish me because I had not minded my mother. Retreating to the back bedroom, the only bedroom, I put up the defense of evoking sympathy by crying on the bed.

I was sorry. Heartily sorry.

I would not do it again. Never. Ever.

Despite my pleas, my mother remained steadfast in her demand for justice without any sense of mercy. My father, almost six feet tall and over two hundred pounds, would engulf me with his right arm, take down my pants and underpants, and with the belt in his left hand repeatedly strike my buttocks and the back of my thighs. I cried but probably my cries were more akin to wails. There is an old vaudeville joke that goes "Why do you keep banging your head against the wall?" The answer to the joke "Because when I stop it feels so good" is what I remember. Suddenly the episode ended. It felt so good not to be hit again. My father released me and I got dressed. The pain slowly evaporated from my thighs, like ebbing sunburn. I didn't sustain any welts or bruises. I wasn't cut and I didn't bleed but the soreness would last. My father possessed an art for this science. My feelings of inadequacy, that I couldn't please my mother or win her back after I did something wrong, colored my personality for many years as I often referred to myself as a klutz. What I remember today and I ask "Was I really that bad a kid to get beaten?" My younger sister and brother maintain this strict parental discipline never happened to them. As the saying goes; the second and third child are raised by different parents.

I wonder where my mother stood while my father inflicted the punishment. I don't remember her watching. Did she stare at me from the bedroom door with her hands folded across her chest? Did she return to the kitchen where it was certain she could hear me wail? How did my father feel being railroaded into the role of disciplinarian? I have the feeling he succumbed to doing his duty. Was he happy with this decision he had no part in making? How many times did he hit me? Were there some rules for the nature of the offense? Five lashes for disrespectful speech? Ten whips for unruly behavior? If either of my parents were alive today, I doubt I would ask them any of these questions. Resurrecting these emotions in them wouldn't be worth the risk of reminding them of what can only be called an act of barbaric child-rearing. The fact that it was all too common in those days didn't excuse it.

Obviously this form of punishment had very little effect on my behavior. If it had, the spankings would not have happened as often as they did. I remember it occurred many times.

For most of us, I imagine, we think of our parents as *our* parents, not as parents. I wish I could engage them now with questions not about the painful particulars of my childhood but about their own experience of being a parent. In his memoir *Growing Up* published in 1982, Russell Baker wisely notes that "Children rarely want to know who their parents were before they were parents, and when age finally stirs their curiosity there is no parent left to tell them." I wish I had read his insights back in 1982 and acted more daring by asking my mother some pointed questions. In her answers I might have appreciated her and my father more for the tribulations they must have endured. The first four years of my life were a time of war and little prosperity. How did they manage to endure and survive?

I would skirt the issue of the spankings hoping they might just talk about it. My parents are no longer alive but if they were I would engage them with questions not about *my* childhood but about their *own* experience of being a parent. Now I would be unafraid to ask them what in my younger years I would have considered "touchy" issues. Now it's too late to walk a mile in their shoes and feel what they felt.

I cannot deny who I was and, in smaller ways, who I am still. I was an irascible child, petulant, quick-tempered; a mischievous child, the model of an imp with a capital 'I.' I was a grocery list of faults. I overturned garbage cans in alleyways and used the tops as shields in sword fights. I propped open the elevator door in my apartment building, preventing its use. I stole penny caramel chocolates from Coyne's Candy Store, and dropped water balloons from the roof of our six storey apartment building. Worst of all, I threw rocks at buses going up Heath Avenue in the Kingsbridge section of the northwest Bronx. I should have had more respect—my father was a bus driver.

If I had virtues, they were submerged under my total lack of self-esteem for much of my early life. I presume that as I grew, to distinguish myself, I was less and less obedient to my mother's commands until she ran out of patience as the saying went in my family. I evidently had very little reserve in the patience department. Whatever I did wrong, whatever sin I committed, I do not remember, but my egregious behavior provided sufficient reason for the wrath of my mother to be vindicated by the belt of my father. It is true that as a child and into my young adult years I was easily upset, quick to anger and volatile to a fault. It would take many years for this vice to subside.

Aristotle has remarked that "Anybody can become angry - that is easy, but to be angry with the right person and to the right degree and at the right time and for the right purpose, and in the right way - that is not within everybody's power and is not easy." I will attest to Aristotle's wisdom—I have been angry many times in my life.

Now I am older and have mellowed but I have not been cured entirely. Fortunately, I never harmed anyone in my fits of temper. My father's beatings (there really isn't another word for them although spanking was the word in vogue then) are probably the saddest memories of my childhood. Perhaps these lingering memories affected my own parental behavior. I don't believe I ever hit either of my children as a form of punishment. Yell and scream, hold and restrain, most certainly, but I can't remember striking them. If I did, I acted impulsively.

I do, however, remember one incident when my children were small. Whatever the reason, I was quite piqued at something one of my children did. As I hustled them into the car, I slammed the passenger door closed so forcefully that the window shattered. Luckily, both of them were safe in the back as glass flew across the front seat. I stood stunned at the damage caused by my own lack of self-control and the realization it might have been worse. During the drive home I concocted a story my wife might believe.

But never have I grabbed a belt or anything else and spanked my daughter or son as a form of corporal punishment. That outburst of breaking the car door glass may have been the moment I started to change, but the mellowing process, like aging wine and whiskey, takes years. I remember reading the last stanza of *Antigone* and thinking several lines apropos.

> "Of happiness the crown
> And the chiefest part is wisdom …
> We learn when we are old."

Better late than never, as they say. I like the expression—break the cycle of pain. I hope I have made the anger link between my ancestors and my progeny weaker.

Children act impulsively. I've seen it in my own children and now I watch it in my grandchildren. Their peaks and troughs of behavior are more pointed than the daily behavior of adults which is smoother and less volatile. A two-year-old child can traverse the emotions of utter disappointment accompanied by howling to a serene peace with a smile in a matter of seconds. A change in the behavior of children is like a baseball coming off a bat. One second the ball is hurtling toward the catcher and the next second it's sailing into the center field bleachers. For most adults the intense 180° transformation would take a night and a day or more.

While I can't remember if the first time I was beaten was on that November day I can distinctly recall the last time I thought it would happen, but didn't.

I was about eight, maybe older. It was a Saturday morning in late August. My parents were packing suitcases for our summer vacation down in Lavallette on the Jersey shore. While they were busy preparing for the two-week holiday, I wondered how I would break the news that at the end of June I had secretly started a newspaper delivery route. Instead of playing in the neighborhood every afternoon, I delivered the *New York Post,* which my family referred to as the "communist" newspaper.

My father bought several newspapers each day: the *Daily News*, the *Daily Mirror*, the *World Telegram and Sun* but never the *New York Times* or the *Post*. I felt I had to tell them; lying was never one of my strong vices. When I did, I was positive I'd be beaten. I waited as long as I could postponing my inevitable revelation. As we are getting in the car, I divulged my secret but there was no immediate repercussion.

Instead, as we started the drive, my father turned right on Bailey Avenue rather than left, and then stopped at the store front on West 231st Street where the papers were unloaded, unbundled, and counted out for the delivery boys. I walked in with my father and he informed the manager that I wouldn't be delivering that day or any other day in the future. My father and the manager conversed cordially for several minutes. I could not hear them; perhaps I was complimented on my work ethic, but I fretted during the entire trip to the Jersey shore. The trip was interminable; there was no New Jersey Turnpike, no Garden State Parkway, and my imagination locked in on how painfully my vacation would start. As we turned off Route 9 at Toms River, New Jersey and headed east to Seaside Heights and Barnegat Bay, I could smell the salt water in the air. Usually that scent escalated my enthusiasm for frolicking in the ocean waves, but that day my dread grew. When we arrived I figured I'd get another beating, this time for deception and abetting communism, but the spanking never came. Perhaps my parents secretly admired my resourcefulness. Perhaps what the manager told my father saved me. It would be hard to punish me for behavior that someone's already praised. That day marked my stepping over that threshold separating child from boy. The spankings had stopped.

Chapter 2

According to my baby book, I was born on Sunday, August 17, 1941 at 11:10 A.M. at Westchester Square Hospital. My mother noted that the hospital was in New York City but it's really in the east Bronx. The Bronx, as most people know, is a parallel universe to the rest of New York City. The delivery doctor was E.J. Murphy and the nurse was R. McCoy. I remember none of it.

I write this half jokingly since the many details of my first six birthdays are noted in my baby book and after reading these memories I'm convinced I should remember much of it.

One of my earliest memories is when I was about three years old. I am dressed in a navy blue sailor suit and my mother is snapping pictures with a Kodak Brownie camera. My mother should have been a photographer for my childhood is well documented. In numerous pictures I am immaculately outfitted in what might best be described as a tuxedo for tots. My first photograph was snapped on October 15 almost two months after I was born. That's fairly unthinkable today when the earliest pictures of a baby are mere seconds after birth right in the delivery room. I am perched on the shoulder of someone who isn't identified, but my mother noted that it took place in my grandmother's apartment and that I resembled my father. In the background, there is a fake fireplace and on the mantel is a photograph of a man. I don't know who it is but I think it is my maternal great-grandfather. I wish I knew. I know little of my grandparents and even less of my great-grandparents.

Not only did my mother snap pictures on festive occasions but my father bought a Bell and Howell 8mm camera and the clips that have survived show my mother insisting I do another take for the camera and me shaking my head in disgust.

The early summer months of 1941 must have been tense for my mother. She's pregnant and I wonder if she had any regrets about bringing a new child into a world soon to be plunged into war. The United States was on the verge of entering the European conflict and in a few short months the Japanese Air Force would attack the military base at Pearl Harbor and the war would spread into the Far East. It is only now I want to ask my mother, "What was it like when I was born?" Now I realize the summer of 1941 was filled with anxiety; to enter a war or not must have been the dinner topic at many tables. Did my father enlist? Was he drafted?

None of these events about my father's naval service are clarified in my baby book and the question arose in my mind as to the absence of these details when my mother recalled so many other events. Was there something amiss that my mother chose not to document?

Soon my father would be absent from my young life and my mother, away in the Pacific theater on a Navy ship as a radio operator. As a child I remember vividly his mystical tapping out the Morse code on the kitchen table as he chanted "dah-dit-dah-dah-dit" and thinking his fingers were possessed. With such delicate fingers he might have been a violinist. When my father served in the navy I wonder how my mother felt. What did she worry about? Obviously my father lived to return; many didn't. How did she live; where did the money come from?

On occasion, when my mother was still alive, I mentioned an odd memory I have of the war. I was about five years old. In the parlor—we didn't call it the living room—behind the pull-out couch was a long, thin, cardboard box. I used to stand on it to see over the back of the couch. One day I peeled off the tape and opened it. Inside was a Japanese bolt action rifle, and a pamphlet with instructions, I presumed. I closed the box and pressed the tape back into shape. Many years later, when I mentioned this memory, my mother denied there was any such box. I did not argue there was a box—but there was a box.

Other notes in my baby book are equally mysterious. On the inside front cover is an inscription in my mother's handwriting that the book was a gift from Eileen Brown. I have no recollection of her. Who was she? A neighbor? A childhood friend of my mother's? Did they have a falling out? Did she die, move away? I have little real knowledge of my parents' friends and the ones I know about were my mother's friends, not my father's. I can't ever remember my father mentioning any person he served with in the Navy.

Some events in the baby book are poignant and I would love to ask my mother about my first birthday. She notes I first walked on my first birthday. Does she remember the day? Was my father there? Did she think it was a wonderful birthday present for *her*?

I was not breastfed. It may have been the custom of the times. In my baby book my mother notes that my first bottle was in the hospital. Did she purposely choose that or was she unable to breastfeed. Of course, if my mother was alive and I did ask these questions, she would probably dismiss them immediately as inappropriate. My mother was not one to openly talk of bodily functions.

At first, from my mother's reporting, I was a quiet child. She wrote that I "would not make any attempt to say some words." Then, after a vacation at the shore (Lavallette, New Jersey) I just "said everything." My mother was in awe. She continued, "It was amazing to hear him." It was prophetic sign. In my professional life I made my living talking—I was a teacher.

I wish that she were alive so I could remind her of what she wrote and have her remember that summer, my babbling and her pure delight. I would bring out my baby book from the bottom drawer of my bureau and page through it in the living room and recreate those happy days again. Atticus Finch, in Harper Lee's only novel *To Kill a Mockingbird,* remarks that "You never really understand a man until you consider things from his point – until you climb into his skin and walk around in it." How many people have tried to understand their parents as parents, not *their* parents, but just parents?

On September 14, 1941 I was christened by Father Clement Krug with the name Thomas. It's a fitting name; for much of life I doubted myself and treated much of the world with cynicism. My middle name is Howard. I was named after my father with our first and middle names reversed. My father's brother's wife, Adelaide Brennan, was my godmother and my mother's youngest brother, Edwin Lyons, was my godfather.

I always thought I acquired my penchant for irritability and anger from my father but now I think it's more of a Lyons family characteristic. Other than the occasions of my father spanking me I can't remember him being angry or upset. Even the spankings might have been done out of duty or loyalty to my mother rather than his own anger or disappointment with me.

Some of my memories suggest he might even be happy-go-lucky. One Fourth of July he brought home firecrackers from work. The two of us went to the empty lot next to our apartment house, and he taught me how to blow up tin soup cans. He didn't hear the cops calling him from the squad car that had pulled up to the curb. My mother watched us from the kitchen window and when she saw the cops she called to my father, "Howard! Howard!" With the din of the explosions he didn't hear her either, and only when the cop called out "Howard" did he realize they were there. My father got a stern lecture about bad example and the cops got the remainder of the firecrackers.

Perhaps I inherited my anger from my maternal great-grandfather, the man in the photo on the fake fireplace. My regret is that I never inquired about him or wondered about him until now when it is too late and there is no one alive to answer my questions. The photograph is long lost.

Anger wandered around the family searching for fertile ground. It rooted well in the personality of my Uncle Timmy, my mother's brother, the middle child in their family. He dampened most family gatherings: cold, demeaning and demanding. Recently at a family wedding, I watched my Uncle Timmy's oldest son. Chip off the old block doesn't do justice to his behavior. He was his father's clone.

The wedding was his own son's by his second marriage, a loud, boisterous affair with a disc jockey and a truckload of amplifiers. Recently, I had learned Timmy had been diagnosed with cancer. I walked over to him to make small talk and be sympathetic. Immediately he excused himself saying he didn't feel well. He walked outside and I followed him like a detective. I knew he wasn't sick at all but he was upset—about what I didn't know. He seethed with anger; I knew the emotion too well not to recognize it even as he tried to hide it. He paced, turned around and paced some more, almost ready to explode. He restrained himself but I was sad that I couldn't share with him my own journey out of anger and into tranquility and wisdom.

I admit I don't know him well but my cousin's life seems joyless and barren. He left home at an early age and married quickly. I have often thought he wanted to get away from his father. After several years he divorced. His children are estranged and, despite the miserable experience of his first marriage, his second marriage also collapsed. I often think that could have been me and the remark attributed to St. Augustine echoes in my head. "There but for the grace of God go I."

It may have been that my mother was angrier than my father but she contained it under her veneer of civility. My mother was demure and could have easily passed as aristocratic. Her most egregious fault was she thought she was privileged, and while not adverse to hard work she had an air of expectancy; the good things in life would be provided. It is no surprise that my father worked a lot of overtime.

I can't quite remember when this prickly edge to my personality mitigated but as it ebbed life became more agreeable. Events that might have bothered me immensely or people who crawled under my lean skin I now treat as mere inconveniences and quickly neglect them. There is a phrase, whose origins are in a story about how King Solomon learned that his riches and fortune were transitory; "This too shall pass." I wish I had learned that wisdom earlier in life. My father never got the chance to learn it later in his life. He died a month before his fifty-first birthday. Perhaps it was the stress of the overtime hours at work and the anxiety of living from paycheck to paycheck that took a toll on his heart. His diet lacked balance. Despite the cost, we used butter rather than margarine. Some mornings he ate a T-bone steak topped with two fried eggs.

So far, I have outlived him by twenty-four years and I remember vividly the years, then the months and finally the days as my fifty-first birthday approached. When it finally occurred it was an event to be celebrated; I had outlived my father.

I pray often that my children will acquire wisdom sooner than I did by realizing that the fruit doesn't fall far from the tree. The fruit will fall but I wish it would roll a bit farther into the open meadow. As I was like my father or my uncle, my son and daughter are like me and my grandchildren will most probably inherit the family trait of impatience. A remark attributed to Evelyn Waugh goes "Don't hold your parents up to contempt. After all, you are their son, and it is just possible that you may take after them." If I had only known myself better and earlier in life I probably would have caused a lot less pain to a lot fewer people.

After World War II my father got a job driving a bus. He worked a lot of overtime runs and often came home just before I went to bed. He continued his ritual of putting everything in his pockets inside his cap except he might have some miniature Hershey bars he bought for a penny in the small vending machines in the subway. He'd give them to me as an extra dessert, and rather than chew them I'd let them melt in my mouth so they'd last longer.

My mother would keep his meal warm by preparing a "hot plate." She took a dinner plate and used it as the cover for a pot of boiling water. On the plate she'd dish out my father's portion of the meal and then cover it to keep it warm.

At first he drove a bus for the Baltimore and Ohio Railroad transferring passengers from a waiting station at Columbus Circle in New York City to the trains downtown at Penn Station on thirty-third Street. Later he worked for the Fifth Avenue Coach Company until it went bankrupt in 1962 and was absorbed into the present New York City Transit Authority.

I remember one morning he announced that I would not be attending school but instead accompany him to work. This departure from the daily schedule impressed me as highly unusual. How my mother agreed to this absence I don't know, but my father realized the opportunity he would have that morning might not come again. I was curious about why he was taking me with him but didn't ask any questions. I was happy to miss school, and if any of the nuns had questions about my absence from school my parents would have to answer to them.

That morning we took the #1 IRT subway from 231st Street in the Bronx down to Columbus Circle at 59th Street. In the waiting room I sat on one of the long oak benches while my father went to the garage to get the assigned bus. A few moments later he drove around Columbus Circle and planted me in the right front seat. My feet hardly reached over the edge of the plush cushioning. After several minutes of sitting there alone in the fanciest bus I'd ever been in, the bus started to fill with men I can only recall as being gigantic because most of them were taller than my father as they passed me and sat down. They carried baseball gloves, bats, and bags of balls. It was the entire Washington Senators team, a team so bad the Yankees, and most other teams, regularly beat them. I knew only one name on their roster, Ed Yost who played third base, and I wondered which one he was. In those days I listened to baseball on the radio and read the scores in the newspaper. I had no idea what he looked like. This was the opportunity; my father's assignment that morning was to drive the team to Penn Station where they would catch a train back to Washington, D.C.

Baseball fans in those days recited a little jingle about the Senators; "Washington—first in war, first in peace and last in the American League." Terrible team or not, my father realized passengers like this for a kid who loved baseball didn't come along very often. Unfortunately, there were no autographs, no pictures. Where was my mother that morning with her Brownie camera when I needed her? Where was my father's Bell & Howell?

Sports, especially baseball, occupied much of my childhood although here also I was the dissenter. My father rooted for the New York Giants while my allegiance was to the Yankees. My brother Bobby aligned with my father and rooted for the Giants with such loyalty that even after they abandoned New York for San Francisco, they remained his team. Like every other kid in the Bronx from the 40s and 50s, if I had my stuffed shoeboxes with all my baseball cards I'd be rich.

In 1953 my father worked for the Fifth Avenue Coach Company when the drivers went out on a 29-day strike. Money got tighter and milk tasted different. One morning before breakfast I finally caught my mother mixing powdered milk with water and refilling the glass milk bottles.

My mother got a job as a secretary for a Wall Street broker that provided the income for our family. How she obtained this job I don't know and it's another one of those questions that will remain unanswered. If she received any stock tips she rarely acted on the advice, but the truth is, in my family there was no such thing as investment money. I don't think my father understood the financial world and what he did know he didn't trust. Our bank was the kitchen table; my parents had no checking account. They kept a stack of #10 envelopes between the salt and pepper shakers. Each one was labeled: rent, food, telephone, electricity and vacation. No envelope existed for clothing. When I got a new pair of dungarees a tight belt kept them on my hips and the cuffs were rolled up to my shins. The family finances were predominately cash although my mother maintained a "Christmas Club" account at the North Side Savings Bank on 231st Street and encouraged me to start one so I could buy presents in December.

Occasionally, I was entrusted with paying the rent for our one-bedroom one-bathroom apartment. The rent for the month was stashed in its allotted envelope, and I would bring it from our fourth floor apartment down to the basement where Mr. Johnson, the "super," lived. He was a light-skinned Negro with streaks of gray through his short curly hair, and when he opened the door to his apartment I handed him the envelope. He took it and returned into his apartment to record the payment but left the door ajar. I moved closer to the threshold and peeked in. I saw a neat apartment, comfortably furnished, with end tables covered in doilies just like in my apartment but the cooking aromas differed. I heard another voice, presumably his wife, who I rarely saw.

His job, for which he lived rent free, was to be the caretaker of the apartment building. He repaired electrical outlets, arranged for apartments to be regularly painted, adjusted broken radiators on cold mornings, maintained the coal furnace and collected the rent. Despite what pejorative names other boys might call him, my father made clear to me I was always to refer to him as Mr. Johnson. The terms "black" and "African-American" were still far in the future, and referring to him as "colored" or worse was, in my family, as bad as any four letter word. In our neighborhood Irish families predominated with a sprinkling of Italian and German and one or two Jewish families. But the Bronx of the late 1940s and early 50s, while not technically segregated, symbolized the theory of separate but equal.

I distinctly remember that my father had a fondness for Mr. Johnson and would engage him in conversation. My father, like many bus drivers, was gregarious and anxious to chew the fat anybody offered him. He must have gotten along with the blacks who also worked for the Fifth

Avenue Coach Company. At his wake, one of them appeared at the door of Williams Funeral Home on Broadway near West 233rd Street. Most of the mourners didn't quite know what to do when they saw a black man walk into an Irish wake, and it must have taken more than a bit of courage on his part, not only to walk through a white neighborhood alone, but to come at night. I noticed he was wearing a bus driver's uniform and in his hand he held his motorman's cap. I approached him and introduced myself as my father's oldest son. He told me he worked with my father and had come to pay his respects to Howard but that he wouldn't stay long. I escorted him to the casket. He said a prayer and the next moment he was gone. I don't remember his name nor did I ever see him again.

Many years later I came upon an article in The New York Times that chronicled the retired lives of blacks who worked for the Fifth Avenue Coach Company. They meet annually in Rocky Mountain, North Carolina. In the article, one man, who started working in 1967 (three years after my father died) remarks that he "was working [as a union representative] under an Irishman."[1] The union chairman only catered to the Irish from the old country but his disposition alienated the young American Irish who, at the next union election, voted the Irishman out and installed the first black union chairman at the Kingsbridge Depot in Manhattan. I believe that my father practiced civility long before civil rights became the law on July 2, 1964. The list of questions I now have about his job and the people he worked with is extensive. What conversations we might now have, what memories we might enjoy. But it will not happen. On June 1, 1964, one month before the Civil Rights Act was passed my father died; it was my mother's fiftieth birthday. This intertwining of my father's death on my mother's birthday did eventually pass, but it took a long time before June 1 was again a celebration rather than a memorial.

My mother lived another thirty-five years, never remarried, never even considered it I think; one of those questions that, if asked, she would quickly dismiss. She died on August 25 at the age of eighty-five, three days before what would have been her sixty-first wedding anniversary and, I believe, took many family secrets to her grave.

Despite my mother's death I still harbored a curiosity about my father, especially his naval service, so I wrote to the Military Personnel Records of the United States Navy and requested my father's records. Paging through them I learned the name of his training ship, the USNTS Samson, his training locations in Newport, Rhode Island, Little Creek, Virginia, and Lido Beach, New York. My son, coincidently, lived for a while about a mile from where my father went to war on the U.S.S Winston. In the same vein, my daughter also lived a mile from where my wife grew up. I wonder if there is something about my family heritage that calls my children back to certain places in their parents' and grandparents' lives. Is there a gene that acts like a homing device?

Continuing through the records I discovered that my father was in Japan during the immediate American occupation from September

27 to 30, 1945 where he "participated in the occupation of Japan at Wakayama, Hiro Wan and Kure" and again on October 22, 1945. For this service my father earned the World War II Victory medal. I had never heard of this and I discovered more good news. My father was eligible for other medals: the American Area Campaign Medal and the Asiatic-Pacific Area Campaign medal.

My thoughts returned to that Japanese rifle my mother denied ever existed. Was she lying or did she forget or was the possession of the rifle considered contraband? I never heard about any medals for my father when I was growing up.

However, it is inevitable that in rummaging around the closets of history there is also bad news to be unearthed. In his naval record there is a simple form entitled "For Use of Men Inducted Into Naval Service." There are three questions on the form. The first question is "Have you ever been arrested or in the custody of the Police?" My father wrote his answer in his bold left-handed script—"Yes." It took me a moment to recover from my shock before I continued reading his explanation. "Grand larceny 3 times. Dismissed 2 times. Suspended sentence petty larceny."

Well, I thought, perhaps these events were all a misunderstanding and everything turned out alright. My Pollyanna take on my father's crimes soon dissolved when I read the second question. "Have you ever been in a reform school, jail, or penitentary (sic), or have you ever been convicted of a crime?" Again, in my father's hand he answered—"Yes."

The third question was anticlimactic. "Are you now on probation?" No.

I still disbelieved—the Navy had sent me the wrong records—so I brought out my eighth grade report card from St. John's which my father signed rather than my mother. He also signed the bottom of the navy form. I lined up the two signatures—"Howard T. Brennan." Over the years from thief to parent he had put a slight flourish on the middle initial.

My sister told me she knew nothing about this, my brother is long dead and my only living aunt, the widow of my mother's brother couldn't shed any light on my father's crimes. The sad thing for me is that while I now know more facts about my father's life I don't know if my mother ever knew anything about my father's criminality. These questions remain in the unanswerable category. In the search for my family history I had walked up to the edge of a gigantic sinkhole. I peered in and saw no bottom to the void.

Chapter 3

After World War II my father returned home from the navy. He had served almost two years from New Year's Eve 1943 until November 5, 1945. I entered kindergarten on September 16, 1946, and began to grow up Catholic. By the time third grade rolled around my school day followed a predictable schedule. I got up in the morning, washed, dressed—I took a weekly bath on Saturday night in preparation for Sunday Mass—ate breakfast and walked to school. Getting dressed meant wearing a uniform for my Catholic grammar school, St. John's on the corner of Godwin Terrace and Kimberly Place in the Kingsbridge section of the northwest Bronx. Black shoes, blue pants, white shirt with a clip-on blue tie. Attending a Catholic school not only demanded conformity in belief but also in dress.

My breakfast consisted of cold cereal; Wheaties, (I would study the portraits of baseball players on the front of the box), Cheerios, and Rice Krispies. I topped my cereal with sliced bananas while my father ate a bowl of unadorned

Post Grape Nuts. I watched him shovel the brown nuggets into his mouth and thought he was eating a bowl of small screws drowning in milk. I needed to eat my cereal quickly before the milk seeped into the porous flakes turning them into a mound of mush. The tiny Grape Nuts—a misnomer, I thought, the cereal had neither grapes nor nuts—could sit in the bowl all morning and retain their diamond solidity. Milk was only pasteurized, not homogenized, and I always tried to be the first one to use an unopened bottle of milk so I could pour the cream at the top of the bottle into my cereal bowl.

For several years an unseen milkman delivered two quart glass bottles and left them at the front door of our fourth floor apartment—4F. Quaint customs, like home milk delivery, would soon pass into lore, but I can remember several peddlers plying their trade up Heath Avenue.

There was the vegetable man, his hand firmly on the bridle of a horse pulling a wagon full of produce. He posted the prices on brown bags stuck on sticks attached to the wooden frame that ran down the middle of wagon. My mother would wrap a dollar bill around a quarter and toss it to me from the kitchen window. I knew what fresh produce to buy (potatoes, onions, lettuce and tomatoes) and what not to buy (leeks, Brussels sprout, kale) and if my mother changed her mind she leaned out the kitchen window and yelled a new order down to the peddler.

There were other wagons. I watched sparks fly as the "scissor man" sharpened knives on a manual grindstone he pumped with his feet. Burly men with ice picks fashioned blocks of ice on flat bed trucks. They hoisted the ice to their shoulders and delivered it to the less affluent who still owned ice boxes instead of refrigerators. Our entire apartment building was heated by a coal furnace in the basement. When there was a delivery, the coal shot down the chute from the truck into the coal bin, and I'd hang around and steal the chunks that fell onto the sidewalk. During the year my parents suggested Santa Claus would replace gifts in my Christmas stocking with a lump of anthracite if I misbehaved. That threat lost its effectiveness when one Christmas Eve my father confessed to the lore of Santa. After my brother and sister had been put to bed, my father astonished me with a brand new baseball glove, a ball and a bottle of linseed oil. He placed the glove and ball with the rest of my presents under the Christmas tree and instructed me to act surprised on Christmas morning. I spent the entire month of January rubbing the oil into the pocket of the glove, and imagined myself scooping up ground balls effortlessly at shortstop that spring although, on my Kingsbridge Little League team, I often played right field where hardly a ball was ever hit. When a left-handed hitter came to bat the coach moved me to left field. I only had talent in my imagination.

One peddler offered his wares exclusively to the children—the yo-yo man. Each spring he appeared with his box of yo-yos and demonstrated his tricks: walk the dog, cat's cradle and up the ladder and ambidextrous tricks using two yo-yos simultaneously. If I had saved enough of my allowance I purchased an exclusive yo-yo with embedded rhinestones.

Those were the days when doctors made house calls. The two major drugs of the 1950s were aspirin and penicillin and when Salk made his discovery for preventing polio, my mother breathed a sigh of relief. Polio was a word on the tip of my mother's tongue. One of the most frightening photos I can remember as a child was in *Life* magazine, showing a boy lying in an iron lung staring at the camera with vacant eyes. It depressed me that he could never play baseball.

Like most small children I got sick. Ten days after I was vaccinated in September 1945 (probably for smallpox) I developed a fever and an inflammation on my leg. The following February, 1946 I caught the "grippe." My mother confined me to bed for a week, February 12 through the 18. One night I had a temperature of 104°. My mother noted many of my childhood illnesses: I caught the measles in February 1946, the mumps in February 1947 and, despite the vaccination, the chicken pox in January 1948.

My parents' attitude to medicine included a shaman's belief in the efficacy of enemas to relieve a fever, and I still shiver at the memory of being sprawled over the edge of the bath tub and having the rubber tube shoved up my rectum. No wonder one of the most vitriolic remarks spewed by kids during my childhood was "go shove it up your ass."

Fortunately my mother kept detailed records, not only in my baby book but in supplementary notes, because the uneducated medical treatment I received in the early 1940s would lead to a serious predicament later in my life.

On November 13, 1941 when I was three months old, my mother copied a letter that Doctor Samuel Richman, a specialist with an office on Park Avenue, had sent to our family doctor, Doctor Eusebius Murphy, about my condition after my thymus was x-rayed. The note reads that I had a "radiographic examination of the chest ... and there is a definite widening of the superior mediastinum." The note continues with the following diagnosis. "The radiographic characteristics are those of a moderately enlarged thymus." I was given three x-ray treatments during late November and early December, 1941. On December 11, 1941 Doctor Richman reports that the size of my thymus is within normal limits. My mother tucked the notes inside my baby book, but the memory of my illness lingered in her mind.

Thirty-two years later she read and saved an article from the November 1973 issue of the *Readers Digest* titled "I am Joe's Thymus" and added it to the doctor's notes. She worried more than I realized. In the January 19, 1976 issue of *U.S. News and World Report* in the section of the magazine called "News You Can Use" she read the following paragraph.

Warning to Radiation "Victims:" To people who had radiation therapy to shrink infected tonsils, adenoids or thymus glands as children during the 1930s, '40s and '50s: tell your doctor or hospital as soon as possible....It has been discovered that the radiation treatment, discontinued 20 years ago is related to a high incidence of cancer of the thyroid.

My mother heavily underlined the words "thymus glands." She showed me the articles and the actual letters she received from those doctors. At the same time she gave me my baby book for safekeeping.

Several months later Dr. James Hurley of the Division of Endocrinology at New York Presbyterian Hospital examined my thyroid. He was fascinated with the letters and my mother's handwritten notes from a less enlightened era of medicine, but he found no cancer. He photocopied the letters and the notes so he could use them when teaching other doctors.

On a subsequent visit he asked me to hang around. Later, we went to a classroom and he used me as a model demonstrating how a doctor should probe around my glands and neck searching for thyroid cancer. He pushed my Adam's apple and massaged my glands and I am positive he could choke a person to death in less than five seconds. I elected to kill my thyroid and will take the synthetic hormone Synthroid every day for the rest of my life.

ଙ୍ଗ

St. John's, like all Catholic grammar schools, was less an educational institution and more a little monastery for children. The most important subject was religion and the bible wasn't *the* Bible at all but the neatly framed book of one hundred questions with infallible answers called *The Baltimore Catechism*. Learning religion meant memorizing and reciting answers to questions I would never have thought to ask, questions so profound that even today they sound inscrutable.

In the history of philosophy there has never been any agreement on the correct answers, if there are any, to any of the first three questions in the catechism: Who made the world? The catechism answer is direct; "God made the world." It was as simple as that. There was no follow up question as to how He made it or why.

The second question expands on the first answer: "Who is God?" The answer is equally simple; "God is the Creator of heaven and earth, and of all things. "

The third question is similar: Who is man? "Man is a creature composed of body and soul, and made to the image and likeness of God." The Baltimore Catechism did not concern itself with ontological questions.

For me, memorizing the answers was the pinnacle of boredom until the lesson hit question fifty-nine; "What are the chief sources of sin?" I found the information valuable and the answer of "pride, covetousness, lust, anger, gluttony, envy, and sloth" seemed interesting items to investigate. I already understood anger but remember covetousness as mysterious. What was there to covet? Every family on my block in the Bronx had pretty much the same things. One family's possessions didn't differ much from another. Perhaps the families with iceboxes coveted our refrigerator.

Lust, essentially, was the desire to page through the magazines hidden under the counter in Coyne's Candy Store and with my father's dedication to overtime, sloth was never a temptation. In fact, hard work seemed attractive.

From kindergarten to sixth grade my teachers were nuns, often called sisters, but the religious order at St. John's, the Religious of Jesus and Mary, called the nuns mothers. They had two first names: Mother Mary Theresa, Mother Mary Catherine but some were unfortunate enough to be named after men—Mother Mary Joseph, Mother Mary Peter or Mother Mary Regis.

Mother Mary Theresa, my fourth grade teacher, was a distant relative of my mother, something like a second cousin once removed, so I think my mother had an ear to the ground in case I should continue my disobedient ways at school. The nuns, like my parents, also believed in corporal punishment and often wielded the ruler across my bare palm or knuckles.

Nuns in the middle of the 20th century, it turned out, weren't very educated themselves. Some had no more than a high school education or maybe one year of college, so the curriculum emphasized subjects that could be taught by rote: correct spelling, the intricacies of fractions, the memorizing of state capitals and the Baltimore Catechism. If school time needed to be filled, an extra lesson in perfecting our handwriting according to the Palmer Method would suffice. Underneath the dominating crucifix in every classroom were the perfectly formed letters of the alphabet strung around the classroom like banners. My father was a natural lefthander—his nickname as a child was Lefty—and when he was a child, he told me, they tied his left hand behind his back in an attempt to force him to write with his right hand. He never converted.

One morning in the fourth grade, fidelity to my fidgety character proved my undoing. The only writing instruments permitted by the nuns were the #2 pencil and the ink pen. Ball point pens were expressly forbidden. Each desk had a compartment underneath for storing books and a glass inkwell sat in a hole at the upper right-hand corner of the desk. The bottom of the inkwell could be pushed up from underneath so it could be removed and refilled and I must have pushed it up a bit too hard. The inkwell popped up like a jack-in-the-box and turned upside down spilling the ink across the desk and down the hole onto the shelf underneath. Some of the ink was absorbed by the pages of the books but some dripped onto my pants. The only thing I could do was to use my hands and try to push the ink back. Since ink isn't absorbed by the skin I wiped my hands on my pants but my plight mirrored the proverbial story about the Dutch boy sticking his finger in the dike; the ink kept coming. I thought it was the modern equivalent of the miracle of the loaves and fishes; two ounces of ink multiplied into two gallons.

I remember Mother Theresa as a genial person. She smiled broadly from deep within her pleated wimple—she was the kind of person who saw good everywhere—but she suppressed a laugh as she approached my desk to investigate my restlessness. The sight of me covered in blue ink was vintage slapstick. She sent me home immediately and she must have made a warning phone call—my mother was expecting me. I don't remember my father finding out. My behavior this time may have been too much for even him and I guess my mother felt my humiliation to be punishment enough. Walking home that morning along 231st Street dappled in blue ink, I felt like a leper. Of course, my friends told me later, I missed the second act where the janitors had to clean up the entire mess.

About this time, 1950, our family, like most Catholic families of the day, outgrew our apartment. My sister, Jean Elizabeth, Jeannie as she was called, was born in July 1945 and my brother Robert Francis, Bobby, a little over two years later in September 1947.

The custom in my family was to shorten the given name so that it ended either with the letters 'ie' or the letter 'y.' My Thomas became Tommy, my brother's Robert became Bobby, my uncle Edwin became Eddie, my uncle Timothy became Timmy and when his first son was born he was known as Little Timmy and his father became Big Timmy.

My sister just missed being an official baby boomer by six months although the term had yet to be coined. We never anticipated that the end of World War II would bring the largest increase in the birth rate ever known in the United States. My family like many others experienced the growth.

With five people in a one bedroom apartment my parents shuffled the sleeping arrangements. My sister slept with my mother on the pull-out couch in the parlor, my brother and I in the bedroom in separate twin beds and my father on a roll-away cot at the foot of the twin beds. With two bureaus, a night table and a cedar chest I could hardly move around the bedroom.

It all seemed normal to me but my parents harbored other plans. They bought a car, a four door Chevrolet, that I remember thinking was foolish. Why would you need a car when you could travel to anyplace you wanted on a bus or the subway? We used the car to go on summer vacation but most of the time it sat parked on Heath Avenue. This soon changed. My sixth birthday, August 17, 1947, was a Sunday. The entry my mother made in my baby book is revealing. "Had a family party. Went riding in the afternoon looking for a house in Jersey." Many similar Sundays followed.

The first decision had been made; it would be in New Jersey. My Uncle Timmy had recently bought one of the first houses built in Levittown on Long Island and my Uncle Steve, my father's brother, bought a 1920s Tudor style home in the Whitestone section of Queens. Buying a house seemed the right economic thing to do. On many Sundays after Mass my father and mother would comb the real estate section of The Daily News, circle a few ads and off we'd traipse to Dumont, Demarest, Englewood, Tenafly and a half-dozen suburban towns just across the George Washington Bridge. My father now worked out of the bus depot on 168th Street and Broadway. Living in northern New Jersey would make his commute quite short.

When we visited the houses for sale I left the realtor's tour and gravitated to one of the bedrooms and dreamed it was mine alone. Some of the bedrooms dwarfed the tiny one in our apartment and every house had at least three bedrooms. My soon-to-be home had both a front and back yard and I believed I might even get a dog but a single family home never happened. My father could never pull the mortgage trigger. The more trips we took to New Jersey, the less likely it seemed that my father wanted to buy a house. There was always some problem.

Fifteen years later, when my father died in the bathroom of our apartment, the only asset he left was a small life insurance policy that probably covered the cost of the funeral and the only cash was what remained in the envelopes on the kitchen table. My parents had paid more than twenty-five years of rent and had no equity to show for it. Had he bought a house and life insurance, my mother's life might have turned out differently.

Later in my life I would decide that I would be different from my father. My financial approach to life would start by buying a house— no matter how financially difficult it might be at the start—and I did. I didn't want to make the same mistakes my father made.

Chapter 4

Several events in the fall of 1953 influenced the next eighteen years of my life.

Not only was my family growing but other Irish families in St. John's parish were as well. A Riverdale Press article my mother stuck in my baby book noted that St. John's School graduated 136 eighth grade students in 1952.[2] This increased to 165 the following year and by the time my class graduated in 1955 the number was 179.

For many years, after the communion at the Sunday masses, the Right Reverend Monsignor J. Scanlan arranged for a second collection and designated the money for "The Building Fund." In his scarlet mozzetta and biretta he stood in the rear of the church at the end of Sunday mass preventing parishioners from leaving until they had contributed to the fund.

In 1947 construction started on a third story to the school building to accommodate the increase of students. Two years later, in late 1949 and into early 1950, he supervised the building of a modern convent for the nuns on the corner of 230th Street and Corlear Avenue. Their former convent, the George H. Moller mansion, directly across the street from the school on Godwin Terrace, would now be known as the "the Brothers' House." Some people continued to call it the convent where the brothers lived.

The brothers were members of the Roman Catholic order of the Brothers of the Christian Schools, a Roman Catholic religious order founded by St. John Baptist de La Salle in 1689 in France. Many male religious orders in the Catholic Church have both clerics who are ordained priests, and brothers, those who do not receive the sacrament of Holy Orders, but only take the vows of poverty, chastity and obedience. The stated mission of the Christian Brothers contained an important premise; the brothers vowed "to teach the poor gratuitously."[3] Members of the Christian Brothers were not priests.

In the late 1940s and early 1950s many parishes in the archdiocese of New York invited the brothers to assume the instruction of boys in their grammar schools. The brothers accepted Monsignor Scanlan's invitation to teach at St. John's.

In the fall of 1950, when I was in the fourth grade, five brothers arrived to teach the boys in the sixth, seventh and eighth grades: Brother George, the principal, Brothers Eugene and Peter who taught the two 7th grade classes and

Brothers Anselm and Walter who taught in the 8th grade. The Kimberly Place side of the school housed the boys' classrooms and a set of double doors separated them from the girls' classrooms on the Godwin Terrace side. The nuns continued to teach the girls.

Brother Luke Salm, the archivist for the New York District of the Christian Brothers, in his essay "A Concise History of the New York District" notes that "In 1950 a new school was opened in St. John's parish in the Bronx in the hope of attracting quality vocations."[4] This was how the Christian Brothers grew; provide a superior education in well-run schools that would attract quality people. I would be one of them.

Many parishes in New York City wanted the brothers to teach in their schools and the brothers, trying to oblige as many parishes as possible, ran short of personnel. This meant that some of the teachers in their schools would be regular persons, primarily women.

In the fall of 1952 my sixth grade teacher was Miss Mary Hagan; it was her second year of teaching at St. John's. While her name sounded prosaic, her teaching wasn't. Her pedagogy indicated that the brothers' style of teaching had influenced her more than the nuns' methodology—and her demeanor wasn't like a nun either. In the sixth grade I had just started to notice girls. In the lower grades when one of the nuns approached my desk to check my work, I smelled the residue of the industrial soap, bleach and starch they used to wash their habits. They kept Borax in business. A white wimple hid many of the facial features of a nun, their ears, chin and half their cheeks but I could see Miss Hagan's full face, her ears, her hair, the curve of her neck, her calves and the thrust of her hips despite the 1950s fashion for women wearing billowy blouses and skirts that reached below their knees. When Miss Hagan hovered over my desk checking my work, I smelled her perfume—it wasn't soap—and learned the nuance between the smell of being clean and the scent of being pretty. I, and I assume most other boys, developed a serious crush on Miss Hagan. If it wasn't for sports I would have thought about her all day.

Only Brother Walter's crush counted. He taught one of the eighth grades, and by the next school year Miss Hagan and Brother Walter disappeared together. I don't remember it being a scandal, primarily because there was nothing scandalous. Brother Walter had only professed temporary vows and he decided not to renew them at the end of the year and was free to withdraw from the order.

In the seventh grade my teacher was Brother Eugene, a lanky man with a stretched neck, sunken cheeks and beady eyes on a face that tapered into a pointed crown on the back of his head. We immediately nicknamed him "the geek" for his odd features. What was also unusual was his teaching; he was a maestro in the classroom.

The nuns' pedagogy consisted in maintaining control by keeping the students busy. The brothers' approach was to keep the students attentive. Brother Eugene expected me to listen first, then take notes and copy his examples from the blackboard.

He upgraded the curriculum of the early grades and made editorial changes on my report card to emphasize the revisions. The class "Spelling," neatly crossed out, was now "English" and "Geography" became "Social Studies." Brother Eugene wrote these words, "English" and "Social Studies," in a perfect Palmer script.

He taught the mathematics class intensely and introduced an activity called "mental arithmetic." Decimals replaced fractions and he emphasized their use in the context of the dreaded "word" problem. He compounded the difficulty; we had to calculate answers without using paper and pencil. During mathematics class he prepared us for "the mental arithmetic contest" to be administered and judged by a neutral third party.

On the day of the contest Brother Eugene introduced Brother Bernard Peter who had what seemed to me a prestigious title, the Auxiliary Visitor of the New York Province of the Brothers of the Christian Schools. The two of them standing in the front of the room made a snapshot of a truly odd couple. Six foot four inch Brother Eugene with thinning hair on his pointed head stood next to Brother Peter, a diminutive man a foot shorter, with a brilliant silver head of hair that must have been molded and kept in place by copious layers of lacquer. Brother Eugene wore the traditional simple black habit that draped to his feet and a clerical collar, the rabat, that looked like two pieces of white Wonder bread stuck under his Adam's apple. Brother Peter wore a black suit, a black vest with a clerical collar whose front was cut into an upside-down "V" to distinguish him from a priest. When he smiled his teeth shone even whiter than his hair, but this man had come for business and his smile and relaxed demeanor proved disarming.

Brother Eugene snapped his fingers. Students stood at attention next to their desks and Brother Peter, without notes, paced the front of the room asking a mental arithmetic question to each boy. His gravelly voice with exquisite enunciation was stunning. No paper and pencils were allowed, just your God-given intelligence, alacrity, and a bit of luck. Those students who hesitated or answered incorrectly sat down and the winner was the last boy standing. Brother Eugene stood aside, like a nervous new father in a hospital waiting room, anxious to see how well he had prepared us, but Brother Peter asked diabolical questions. "What is the decimal for seventeen one hundred thousandths?" "How much is 22% of 4,410?" And Brother Peter wasn't averse to posing trick questions. "Which is greater," he asked: "(a) 35% of 87 or (b) 87% of 35?" Given an (a) or (b) choice, most boys relied on luck, it had to be one of those answers, but the correct answer, Brother Peter announced, was neither; (a) equaled (b). For each wrong answer he chuckled as if to say "You're not as smart as you think you are."

Several rounds later I was still standing. I felt odd towering over the seated students and being singled out, not for what I had done wrong, but for what I done right. While I didn't win it's easy to understand why I started enjoying mathematics.

Religion class also changed. While recitations from the Baltimore Catechism continued, the brothers introduced the books of the

New Testament, particularly the four Gospels. I didn't study them directly but Brother Eugene read selected passages, mostly the stories of Jesus' miracles, followed by commentary. He had, of course, a hidden agenda. When Brother Eugene explained the parable of the laborers in the vineyard from the Gospel of St. Matthew, he elucidated the meaning of the verse "Many are called but few are chosen." This passage, he informed us, not only told the story of men following Christ as His apostles, but contained contemporary meaning—some of us would have vocations to the religious life. He explained the etymology of the word "vocation," it means to be called, and it would not be long before some of us would hear that call to the religious life.

I liked the brothers; they seemed real. The nuns of the Religious of Jesus and Mary were technically semi-cloistered. They could not appear in public without wearing their religious habit. Although Mother Theresa was a relative on my mother's side of the family, the cloistered rules of her religious order forbade her from visiting our apartment. The nuns were circumspect about their behavior and after their teaching day retreated inside their convent. The brothers, after the school day was over, changed from their religious garb to t-shirts, sweat pants and sneakers. They joined us playing basketball in the school gym or roller skating in the playground. They quickly organized roller hockey and basketball leagues, and the best of us got to play teams from the other parishes where the brothers also taught.

I took these games seriously; I played hard and hated to lose. One afternoon during a roller hockey game I cross-checked another player, stumbled, tripped over my hockey stick and landed on my right arm. I got up and wanted to continue playing, but as I gripped my hockey stick I couldn't close my fingers because of the intense pain. I walked home carrying my skates and hockey gloves in my left hand and guiding the hockey stick along the ground with my right arm. When the pain didn't subside I knew it was more than a sprain. My mother, still documenting my childhood, made a note in my baby book on October 6, 1954. "Playing roller skate hockey. Fell on right arm. Very swollen and sore. Went to Medical Center. X-Ray showed arm fractured just above wrist. Six weeks in cast. [By] March 1, 1955. Arm ok."

It wasn't just me; sports dominated our recreational lives. In the graduation issue of the school's newspaper, the *St. John's Eagle,* an entire page is devoted to the athletic tournaments our teams won: the hockey team claimed the Bronx Championship, the varsity basketball team won the Manhattan College tournament and the junior varsity won the La Salle Academy tournament. During the seventh and eighth grades I traveled all over New York City to sports events: the 168th Street armory for the C.S.A. L. (Catholic School Athletic League) track meets, Power Memorial High School on 61st Street, and La Salle Academy on 2nd Street for basketball tournaments.

As for being called to the religious life, I listened very carefully but didn't hear any voices. I was a literalist when it came to religious concepts. Maybe I had missed the voices because I wasn't paying attention or the calls weren't loud enough. How many times would this voice call before giving up? Finally, I decided I must have been called and missed it, so it was that late spring afternoon when I was in the eighth grade, I decided to tell Brother Eugene. I wasn't comfortable informing him in school. Somebody might hear me talking and I wasn't sure being called was good or bad in the eyes of my friends. I had hung around after a softball game and when I thought no one was watching I run up to the front door of a former convent. When the nuns had lived here, we were forbidden to walk through the gate, much less up the stairs to ring the doorbell. When one of the brothers answered, I asked to see Brother Eugene. He invited me in and told me to wait in the parlor.

Brother Eugene soon calmed me. After listening to me profess my belief that I had a religious vocation, he escorted me into the chapel where I prayed silently. One of my fears was Brother Eugene would be able to discern whether or not I had a vocation and come right out and conclude that I didn't. I was relieved that he thought maybe I did have one.

So I started getting up earlier and, without eating anything since I would receive Holy Communion, I hiked across Kingsbridge to the morning mass at St. John's Church on Kingsbridge Avenue. Before mass started, the two dozen nuns filed in from a side door in crisp military style. They entered on the left side of the church, the gospel side as it was known, since a reading from one of the four gospels would be read on that side of the altar. The mother superior snapped a clicker and the nuns sat, stood and knelt in a regimented unison only a drill sergeant could love. The brothers sat on the right, the epistle side of the church. The only other people in the church were four or five women dressed entirely in black, the professional mourners of the parish, who, fingering their rosaries, sat in the rear pews of the church.

The altar boy rang a bell and he and the priest entered the sanctuary. On the mornings when the assigned altar boy failed to show up to serve mass, I took his place. The nuns, being women, were forbidden to do so, and the brothers, as I was soon to learn, had major differences with the clergy in general. I looked around and when no one volunteered I walked up the center aisle, opened the sanctuary gate and joined the priest at the altar. I had all the Latin responses memorized, but if I forgot, there was a cue card on the altar steps next to the consecrations bells.

When communion time came I got a close-up look at the faces of the brothers. At the conclusion of the mass, the priest administered Holy Communion to himself. I went over to the offertory table next to the altar on the right side of the altar, the epistle side as it was called, since the most common scriptural reading came from St. Paul's epistles. I picked up the Communion paten, a circular gold plate about six inches in diameter, returned to the foot of the altar and knelt. The priest opened the tabernacle door, removed the ciborium with the consecrated hosts, genuflected, turned and carried the ciborium to the altar rail where he would distribute Holy Communion to the congregation who knelt at the Communion rail. I followed the priest. As he gave Communion to each person, I stood to his right and held the paten under the person's chin. After each one received the host I proceeded to walk backwards from left to right along the Communion rail to the next person.

I stared right at each person's face. They had to close their eyes and stick out their tongues to receive the host. I studied their tongues; different shades of red with some tongues pointed and some rounded. Some communicants stuck their tongues far out, others didn't, and those with pointed tongues didn't hold the host very well and sometimes the host dropped. I was expected to catch it with the paten.

The trip across Kingsbridge was long and to occupy my mind as I walked to and from mass I started reciting ejaculations, short prayers that were rewarded with indulgences. While the Catholic Church had long since abandoned selling indulgences, it still peddled their accumulation so that the stopover in purgatory on one's way to heaven would be as brief as possible. The marriage of religious ideas and arithmetic calculations led me to examine the quantity of indulgences to be acquired. Indulgences were measured in days and years. I noticed that specific prayers that might take a minute to recite were rewarded with only thirty days indulgence while reciting the four words "Jesus, Mary and Joseph," which would only take two seconds, provided an entire seven years. So, as I walked to mass each morning, I rattled this ejaculation as many times as I could and, since I was reasonably good at mental arithmetic, I calculated that over the course of a month I garnered several hundred centuries of indulgences. My infantile idea of God was essentially that He was the Great Accountant.

It never occurred to me that the nature of the afterlife, heaven, hell and purgatory, was essentially timeless and that temporal days and years wouldn't mean much in the land of eternity. And how could it be that pictures in the daily missal showed bodies burning in purgatory and hell with their hair aflame since it was only our souls that went to these places? Our bodies wouldn't join our souls until the final Resurrection, but burning souls could feel the pain of fire as if they had bodies. It was quite irrational, unfathomable and beyond common sense, but I accepted and believed it all. When faith and reason collided, the Catholic Church embraced faith—reason be damned. Uncertainty, about questions like these, had answers, and if I found them unconvincing I would just have to strengthen my faith. Like the father in the gospel of St. Mark who brought his possessed son to Jesus to be healed, I prayed "I do believe; help my unbelief."

My name is Thomas, and like my namesake I doubted a lot, but to be on the safe side, I continued accumulating indulgences and in case I hadn't accumulated enough, I started wearing the brown scapular, two pieces of cloth, about an inch square, embroidered with a cross and connected by two string necklaces. I wore the scapula over my shoulders, one cloth piece rested on my chest, the other on my back. The literature proclaiming its benefits promised that the Blessed Virgin Mary, under the name of Our Lady of Mt. Carmel, will protect anyone wearing the scapular at the time of death and the wearer will escape the eternal fires.

I continued wearing the scapular and reciting ejaculations, but soon my religious behavior would become even more ardent. With prayer and attendance at daily mass, my vocation would grow ever stronger.

Chapter 5

I can't quite remember exactly the moment when I made my decision but during the spring of 1955 I concluded I had a religious vocation and decided to join the Brothers of the Christian Schools. Perhaps it happened at Mass as I sat directly behind the brothers in church. I felt I belonged with them. During the eighth grade I entertained the idea of being a religious, attended Mass more frequently, imagined myself as a brother and by the middle of the eighth grade a decision had been crafted out of many reflective moments.

My parents rarely displayed the piety of many Catholics. We didn't pray the rosary daily, and my mother considered the only bible in our apartment as an heirloom rather than a book to be read. We ate filet of flounder on Fridays, went to confession on Saturdays and attended mass on Sundays. During the remainder of the week religion hardly mattered—except on Tuesday evenings at 8 P.M. when my father insisted on absolute quiet when he watched the television show *Life is Worth Living*, hosted by Bishop Fulton J. Sheen. Before the show started I had to decide where I would sit. After the show started, my father forbade me to move around lest he miss a word from Sheen's presentation. Sheen railed against communism and my father loved every rant.

Eventually, Brother Eugene spoke to my parents, notifying them of the formalities. Since I was thirteen years old, the Brothers needed my parents' permission so I could attend the Day Juniorate for my freshman year of high school and live in the Juniorate in Barrytown, New York for the last three years of high school. The colloquial word Juniorate combines two words, Junior Novitiate and the brothers called us junior novices but the Juniorate' official name was St. Joseph's Normal Institute.

The Brothers wanted to learn a little about my family, so one evening in the spring, after supper, Brother Eugene and a brother I had not met, Brother Thomas, came to our apartment on 3100 Heath Avenue for a visit. My mother dressed as if she were going to the theater. My father arranged his work schedule so he had no overtime that night.

They arrived about seven o'clock, rang our 4F apartment doorbell in the foyer of the apartment building and my father buzzed them in. A minute later they stepped off the elevator on the fourth floor. Both of them wore the formal religious garb, the black suit, and Brother Thomas wore a wide-brimmed black hat and carried a thin leather briefcase. His official title was Vocation Director of the New York District.

My father ushered them to the living room and my mother served cookies, tea and coffee. The four of them talked while I pretended to do my homework on the kitchen table. Our confined apartment allowed the conversation to creep easily around the corners of doors. What they discussed, and what I heard, wasn't a secret: that September I would attend the Day Juniorate for my freshman year at St. Bernard's High School on 14th Street just off 8th Avenue in Manhattan. The following June I would leave home and go to Barrytown.

During my high school years in the Juniorate I wouldn't be an official member of the Brothers so my parents would be responsible for my finances. Tuition for the Day Juniorate cost $30 a month and the following year when I went to Barrytown my parents paid $40 a month for room, board and schooling. Brother Thomas asked if my parents could afford this amount. They said yes, and I imagine they had already discussed paying for my high school education no matter where I might have gone. My parents never considered my attending a public school. At the end of the evening my parents signed some papers and I was accepted. Everyone agreed—I had a vocation.

I guess some families didn't have the resources to pay tuition but the Brothers didn't consider that a problem. If a boy wanted to join, the Brothers would find a financial way. When Barrytown was built in 1930, mothers of boys who had a vocation formed an organization that raised money for the education of the future brothers. They called the organization the Ladies' Auxiliary. Brother Thomas asked my mother if she would be interested in joining a committee. She accepted and soon assisted in organizing the annual card party, dinner and dance held in the spring at the Hotel Statler on 34th Street in New York City.

My mother played cards weekly. She called the evening "having the girls over" and when my mother hosted the party she set up a card table in the living room where three other women joined her playing canasta well into the night. They arrived just after supper. My mother prepared the popular finger food of the 1950s, celery sticks filled with cream cheese surrounded by olives with a toothpick in each one and she complemented the vegetable platter with Saltines and Ritz crackers. They drank sparingly—"high balls"—Four Roses whiskey splashed with ginger ale on ice.

While I continued my homework on the kitchen table, the girls adjourned to the living room, and closed the door so they wouldn't be disturbed. I could vaguely see them through the lace curtains. Sometimes, after I swore I had finished my homework, my mother allowed me to watch a hand or two but I had to be especially quiet since the card game demanded constant attention. They played canasta with two decks of fifty-two cards plus four jokers. Each initial hand contained eleven cards and I admired their dexterity in keeping so many cards arranged in their fingers. When I was allowed to observe, my mother taught me how to count points, when to pick up the discard pile, when not to and how to meld cards for the maximum number of points. When I got up in the morning I saw the detailed scoring pad still on the table next to the last round of melded cards. Points soared into the thousands. My own experience with cards involved no more than the game of "Go Fish."

My mother loved playing cards and that endeared her to the other mothers in the Ladies Auxiliary. She attended her first card party that spring and for many years after. She saved all the souvenir journals. That first one was dated April 22, 1955; I had not even left home yet. In the 1957 edition my parents made a generous donation and saw their names listed under the category "Lieutenants." Since many of the fathers also assisted in the running of the card party, in 1958 they changed the name of the organization to "The Parents Guild." That year my parents made a larger donation and rose in rank to be listed under "Captains." In 1960 the front cover of the souvenir journal stated that the location of the card party was the main ballroom of "The Statler Hilton" reflecting the recent purchase of the Statler Hotels by Conrad Hilton and my mother now served on the awards committee. In 1961 my father became more involved and he served on the Door Prize Committee.

The meeting of the vocation director with my parents solidified my acceptance into the Brothers. I never had second thoughts and anxiously awaited the time to attend the Day Juniorate. My vocation was common knowledge among the other students at St. John's.

At the end of the eighth grade every student took entrance examinations for several catholic high schools. I wondered what would have happened to me if I didn't have a vocation since I failed every high school entrance test I took: Manhattan Prep, Cardinal Hayes High School and Fordham Prep all sent kind letters of rejection. I remember reading the letters with disbelief; I thought I was smart. Brother Eugene noted on my final report card that I ranked fifth in a class of fifty-one but after reading the form rejection letters I felt I wasn't that bright after all. Of course, I misunderstood and thought the schools rejected me because I wasn't intelligent, but the truth was that all these schools suffered from overcrowding and rejected several students for every one they accepted.

On Sunday, June 26, 1955 I graduated from St. John's. In the final issue of the school newspaper, *The St. John's Eagle,* I am listed as the class reporter for one of the 8th grades and I wrote the one page summary of our years at St. John's. I revealed my anxiety in the opening sentence; "At long last the final month has come for us in St. John's School." When I read the short biography of myself on the next page, I was surprised. The short paragraph stated that "Tom is one of the leaders of the class." This came as big news to me. In the graduation poll taken for the class, my name appears nowhere on any list of the twenty categories ranging from "Most Likely to Succeed," "Most Friendly," down to "Typical Boy." I'm positive Brother Eugene wrote the copy for the biographies and he noted my future. "[Tom] is going to St. Bernard's to train for the Brothers' life." If he did not write the copy, then I had a secret admirer, for being a leader was the last thing I would have thought about myself.

The summer of 1955 passed slowly and I anticipated the start of the Day Juniorate. The concept of the Day Juniorate was new and the first class had started only two years earlier. In the October 5, 1955 edition of *The Beacon*, the school newspaper of the Juniorate, an article notes that the population of the Juniorate rose to ninety-five in buildings designed to house no more than ninety. The Brothers created the Day Juniorate so that during the freshman year of high school, boys with vocations wouldn't hear other calls, mainly from girls, who now represented near occasions of sin. The Brothers clearly stated that I should avoid any association with young persons who wore lipstick and skirts.

But my attendance at the Day Juniorate was delayed because my grandfather, my mother's father, who I called "Poppy," died in the first week of September. I believe that he died suddenly because I don't remember him being in a hospital or even being sick. He died as he lived, a taciturn man I hardly knew. He taught me one useless habit—drumming my fingers on the top of a table to create a marching cadence. To this day when I drum, his face appears before me like a hologram.

The funeral mass occurred on Monday, September 12, 1955, the first day of school in the Day Juniorate. What I do remember was being disappointed at not being in school and having instead to attend a funeral. Already my allegiances were elsewhere.

The next morning I joined Edward Fitzpatrick (Fitzy) and Raymond Fischer, two other students who had been called to the religious life, and travelled to St. Bernard's School. They filled me in on what had happened the day before; the brothers had taught the classes from bell to bell—they even assigned homework. I had the funeral as an excuse.

Fitzy had enjoyed playing practical jokes at St. John's and continued the role at St. Bernard's. When he introduced me the next day, I wondered why the students stared at me in disbelief. I learned that Fitzy had spread a rumor of my athletic prowess; at six feet four inches I dominated every basketball court I played on. The students blamed me for shrinking to four feet nine inches overnight.

As for avoiding girls, I took this suggestion seriously and planned my subway ride home from St. Bernard's. When I got off at my station, 231st Street, I needed to pass Luhr's, a soda shoppe, as it was called, on the southeast corner of 231st Street and Broadway. Its white marble countertops, black iron-grille chairs and red leather booths intimated intrigue and attracted swarms of kids from Kingsbridge, Riverdale and Marble Hill. On Friday afternoons teenagers gathered and ordered ice cream sodas, banana split sundaes, lime rickeys— without the alcohol— and egg creams, a confectionery born in Brooklyn, with neither egg nor cream.

I sat in the first subway car and when the train emerged from the tunnel at Dyckman Street I stood and looked out the front window pretending I was the engineer. When I got off the subway, in order to avoid passing Luhr's, I used the exit at the north end of the station platform where the stairs led to the corner across the street from Luhr's. Late Friday afternoons buzzed at Luhr's as boys and girls paired off for a movie date at the Dale theater on 231st Street or the RKO theater farther north on Broadway. Sometimes someone would see me walking up 231st Street with a load of books under my arms and yell, "What's the matter? No date tonight!" I pretended I didn't hear them but turned my head quickly to scan the crowd.

The boys wore their hair long and swept it back to their nape in a 50s style called the DA, the duck's ass. I sported a close crew cut. Despite my vocation I had a serious crush on Ann Byrne, a girl with long black hair who was unaware of how pretty she was. She lived on the other end of Heath Avenue down near Kingsbridge Road and I would ride my Schwinn bike down there hoping she would notice me. She lived in one of the attached private houses and since her family owned it I assumed she was rich. In the graduation issue of the St. John's school newspaper, the girls, in addition to voting for "most likely to succeed" and other categories wrote comments about each other. The remark for this girl was "angel unawares." She was a real looker and I wasn't the only boy to have eyes for her.

I got up on Saturday morning and went to 6:30 mass. When I passed Luhr's I stopped and looked in the window. The countertops were cleared of glasses and ice cream sundaes boats, the booths were empty and the iron grille chairs were stacked upside down on the top of the tables. A mop stood against the door jamb. Someone had cleaned the floor just before they left. I wondered if the black-haired girl had been there and enjoyed the evening.

St. Bernard's School was really on 13th Street between 8th and 9th Avenues in the Chelsea section of Manhattan, the center of the meat-packing district. A courtyard behind the school connected it to the church on 14th Street and once a week I had to walk through the courtyard to go to confession in the church. As I crossed the courtyard I attempted to construct my list of sins; if I had been reasonably good that week I could always use the standby of "impure thoughts" about kissing and making out with Ann Byrne.

The granite and brick school building, four stories high and wedged between two warehouses, stood alone when it was built in 1873. In the fall of 1955 the first two floors of the school housed the grammar school students of the parish. The third floor accommodated students who, the following year as sophomores, would be switching to Cardinal Hayes High School in the Bronx. The brothers segregated us to the top floor of the building away from everyone else. We started classes earlier in the morning and were the last students to leave in the afternoon.

Once I began high school in the Day Juniorate my days of hanging around on Heath Avenue were numbered. I still rose early to attend mass at St. John's and continued to accumulate indulgences. At mass I sat nearer to their brothers since I felt closer to them and already thought I belonged to the Christian Brothers. The daily trip to St. Bernard's on the IRT #1 subway took nearly an hour from 231st Street to 14th Street. At some stops one or two more Day Juniors joined me: Michael Keegan and Thomas Nearny from Incarnation parish that boarded the subway at

168th Street, Thomas Condon from Ascension parish at 103rd Street and Eamon Coughlin from Holy Name was at the 96th Street station. We copied homework from each other, shuffling papers among ourselves when the subway stopped at a station and we could write without shaking. From the 96th Street station to 14th Street the train changed from a local to an express and sped so fast that the cars swayed and it was impossible to write legibly. Some of my copied homework ended up as mere scrawl.

At the beginning of each class we opened our homework books so they could be checked. Brother Basilian walked up and down the aisles examining our work and when he picked up my homework he pointed to my illegible writing and asked, "You must have copied that on the subway after 96th Street?"

Every morning when I reached the 14th Street station I bought a chocolate doughnut and a Nedicks orange juice. I wouldn't bite into the doughnut but press it slightly between my lips, crack the chocolate icing and pick off pieces with my teeth. The orange juice was more soda than juice with a distinct tart flavor that lingered on my tongue.

The curriculum at the Day Juniorate demanded a lot more study than grammar school. Science classes included lab experiments and arithmetic became algebra. We did every single problem in the algebra textbook. For our social studies assignment Brother Albinus of Mary made us buy *The New York Times* and write summaries of the lead articles. He referred to the *Daily News* and the *Daily Mirror* as the daily rags but I continued reading them because the sport sections contained more statistics.

The main intention of the Brothers was to keep us as busy as they could. Letting us go home early and intermingle with our old friends and their new high school girlfriends would only lead to boys losing their vocation. We ate lunch last at 1 P.M after the students who attended the Cardinal Hayes Annex part of the school returned to class. Classes continued until three o'clock.

During the fall after school we changed into our track uniforms and ran around the tar roof and practiced for the cross country track meets held each weekend at Van Cortlandt Park in the Bronx. In the winter we formed basketball leagues. I returned home about six o'clock, had supper and did as much homework as I could before nodding off at the kitchen table.

Brother Basilian assigned some of us responsible jobs. After lunch I took the money collected at lunch in the school cafeteria to deposit in a bank on 14th Street between 7th and 8th Avenues. Most of the cash was wrapped coins and I lugged the pouches to the bank. The return trip was easier since the pouches were empty except for a deposit slip.

At that time 14th Street sported numerous bar and grilles that served lunch to the men working in the slaughterhouses on 9th and 10th avenues. They opened at noon and by one o'clock a dedicated drinking crowd clinked Guinness glasses and regaled each other with stories before returning to work. One October afternoon as I returned to the school I heard a commotion in one of the bars. I stopped, looked in and saw one of the newest RCA color television sets perched over the bar. The men lined the bar watching a live televised game of the 1956 World Series; the Yankees were playing the Brooklyn Dodgers and it was the first World Series to be broadcast in color. My father had sprung for a black and white TV but a color set was too expensive and this was the first time I had seen one. I was impressed with the brown infield dirt, the green outfield grass and the sharp blue pinstripes of the Yankee uniforms but seeing the game on TV differed from being in the stands—TV just didn't convey the immenseness of Yankee Stadium.

Most Yankee fans had a bad feeling that October that turned out to be justified. Dodger fans always moaned "Wait 'til next year" and this year was next year. It would be the only World Series the Brooklyn Dodgers would win in New York City. I inched closer to the door, quietly asked what the score was, lost track of time and watched two innings. I would have watched more except Brother Basilian came searching for me. He approached me from behind, grabbed my ear, twisted it so hard I thought he might tear it off and dragged me back to school.

"What are you doing?" he asked.

"Watching the World Series," I said. I was sure he thought I had been mugged and robbed. My ear hurt for the rest of the afternoon.

The following week Brother Basilian assigned another student to accompany me so I would return to school on time. By the next week the Yankees had lost the World Series, Brooklyn exalted, and I didn't care what they broadcast on the color TV.

Chapter 6

In June 1956, on the last day of school in the Day Juniorate, Brother Basilian handed me a list of clothing to be brought to Barrytown and an empty army duffel bag that my father gradually filled during the next week. My mother washed and ironed every item of clothing I owned and my father flattened, folded and rolled them until they couldn't be condensed anymore. He must have learned the technique in the navy. Everything I brought to the Juniorate had to be in that duffel bag.

My parents made two exceptions. My father bought me a new baseball glove with a ball wedged in its pocket to maintain the shape. The second, a brand new 35mm camera my mother insisted I have.

My father packed t-shirts, dungarees (as jeans were known in 1956), dress shirts, socks, towels, washcloths, a bathrobe, shoes, sneakers, slippers, galoshes (as boots were known then), ties, underwear, gloves, a heavy winter coat plus a parka; every material possession I owned.

On the last Sunday in June the three of us took the #1 IRT subway to 42nd Street, caught the shuttle across midtown and entered the great hall of Grand Central Terminal. It wasn't difficult to find our meeting place. Similar families of a mother, a father and a boy with an army duffel bag congregated near the west staircase leading up and out onto Vanderbilt Avenue.

As we approached the group, Brother Basilian, now dressed in his formal religious garb, black suit, black shoes and the white collar with the upside-down '∧,' greeted us. His perpetual red face looked more flushed than usual but his smile engaged my parents. I wonder if they had reservations about permitting me to go. They were delivering their oldest child to a man they hardly knew and had met once or twice, probably at the card parties at the Statler Hotel. After my decision had been finalized, neither of my parents ever asked me if I should reconsider. I had chosen a noble profession and they acted proud about it.

Brother Basilian pumped my father's hand, patted his back and made small talk as if they were best friends. He worked the crowd of parents like a politician except he didn't want their vote, he wanted their child.

More boys arrived until there were about forty of us. The army duffel bags disappeared, we said goodbye to our parents and boarded a northbound New York Central Railroad train. No one in my family cried, not my mother nor my father and certainly not me. I had no qualms about leaving home.

In my baby book my mother made a note on September 16, 1946, the day I started kindergarten that harbingered this moment at Grand Central. "[Tommy] was quite anxious to go and liked it very much. A little disappointed that he didn't get homework and has no books." Getting far afield from my family was an undercurrent in my life. I often wondered if I entered the Christian Brothers to punish my father for spanking me or my mother for her complicity in the spankings but I don't think I will know for certain. I do know that I never regretted the decision.

As the train emerged from the tunnel at 96th Street I gazed hard at Harlem, a neighborhood I had heard about but never seen. From the train window it didn't look all that different from my neighborhood, lots of apartment buildings and a few basketball courts. The train rumbled across the East River into the Bronx and when I caught a glimpse of Yankee Stadium a moment of nostalgia seized me; I wouldn't see any Yankee games that summer. As the passenger cars curved around 225th Street I tried to find my grandmother's kitchen window among the dozens of apartment buildings atop the highlands of Kingsbridge. She would surely be watching for that afternoon train.

After my grandfather's death, I had often spent the evening with my grandmother in her apartment in the building across the street from ours. My mother suggested the arrangement so my grandmother wouldn't have to be alone at night.

I spread my homework across her kitchen table and when I wearied of solving algebra problems I turned the chair around to the window and gazed out at the Kingsbridge valley. The apartment buildings on the northern section of Heath Avenue rested on a bluff and my grandmother's apartment on the top floor had panoramic views. To the north I saw the immense parade grounds in Van Cortland Park at 242nd Street; to the south I watched New York Central Railroad turned the bend where the Harlem River Canal connects the Hudson and Harlem rivers at 225th Street. Now, instead of watching those trains I was on one trying to find my grandmother sitting at that same window.

The familiar Marble Hill and Spuyten Duyvil stations gave way to towns I knew little about: Yonkers, Tarrytown, Ossining and Croton-on-Hudson where the engines were switched from electric to steam. I thought I was leaving my insular family and venturing into the wider world. In fact, just the opposite was true; I was entering one of the most confined places I would ever live—a rural, semi-cloistered monastery in a religious order of the Roman Catholic Church. I was joining the Brothers of the Christian Schools. It was June 1956 and I was only thirteen years old. Other than brief summer and Christmas vacations, I would never go home again. The Brothers used the phrase—we were visiting home; we didn't live there anymore.

The school's official name was St. Joseph's Normal Institute. When I arrived in the summer of 1956 I was a member of the twenty-sixth group to study there. Barrytown had been built on hope in 1930, a time in America where hope was the only thing most people had. For many the Great Depression had already started and would only get worse.

Prior to Barrytown, the brothers had maintained the Juniorate and novitiate on the 123 acres they owned in Pocantico Hills, New York. After the surge in vocations in the late 1920s, the facilities quickly proved inadequate. In 1928 more than two hundred boys and brothers lived in a building designed for half that number. Their desire to sell and their neighbor, John D. Rockefeller Jr.'s willingness to buy adjoining land to enlarge his estate, made the transaction easy. Rockefeller and the Brothers negotiated a price of $1, 850,000 for Pocantico Hills and the Brothers persuaded Rockefeller to advance money so that the Brothers could purchase the property at Barrytown. The Brothers immediately bought about three hundred acres in the summer of 1928 for $100,000 and started building.

On July 7, 1930 all the Brothers vacated Pocantico Hills and arrived at Barrytown much the same way I arrived, a quarter of a century later, in the summer of 1956—by rail.

Between Poughkeepsie and Albany, New York, the railroad considered many stations "whistle stops," towns so small and isolated the train didn't even make a regular stop. Barrytown was one of them. That Sunday afternoon as we climbed down the steps of the train, we were greeted by other brothers and boys from the Juniorate. They unloaded our duffel bags from the train onto a flat-bed truck that disappeared up Station Hill Road. We had introduced ourselves on the two hour ride from Grand Central and together we walked up the hill through the no traffic light, one church village of Barrytown. As we reached the top of the hill the terrain leveled off.   Corn stalks, already knee high, waved in fields and a water tower on the far eastern section of the property dominated the landscape.   We turned left onto Barrytown Road, circled back west toward the Hudson River and finally walked through the main gate leading to St. Joseph's Normal Institute, my home for the next four years.

I had been to Barrytown once or twice the previous year on weekend visits from the Day Juniorate but on those occasions had arrived by station wagon late on a Friday night when it was dark so I had never fully grasped the scale of the buildings from a distance.   Walking down the main road the scale of the structures overwhelmed me. Its architecture was Italian Romanesque with red brick imported from Holland and the roof line trimmed with Indiana limestone.   The complex consisted of four buildings, roughly arranged in the shape of a Greek cross: the Juniorate, three stories high, the Novitiate, a four story building, and the third building known as "The Ancients" where the elderly and retired brothers lived in The Holy Family community. These three buildings were connected by narthexes (cloistered stone and glass walkways) to a Spanish mission style church, called the "large chapel."   The stained-glass windows, Stations of the Cross on white-washed walls stretching up to vaulted ceilings imbued it with a monastic tone.   A Kilgren organ dominated the choir loft. Its official name was St. Joseph's Normal Institute but everyone just called it Barrytown.

A fifth building, an estate house built in 1886 called the Aspinwald Estate, stood mostly empty. The flaking bricks needed re-pointing and the slate roof sagged; the brothers used the building for storage.

A football field in the front of the Juniorate stretched its entire length and there were two baseball diamonds, one at each end of the football field. Two full size basketball courts, six three-walled handball courts and two tennis courts sat at the south end of the Juniorate. For a boy like me, excited about sports, it was paradise.

On the north side of the Juniorate several statues (St. Patrick, St. Michael the archangel) circled the picnic tables under a grove of pine trees. Farther to the north the brothers maintained a vegetable garden, a cemetery and a working farm: several barns with cows, pigs, and a coop full of chickens and another house where the farm employees lived with their families.

The main order of business was settling in. We entered the Juniorate at the south stairwell and climbed three flights to the top floor, turned left at the top landing into the south dormitory. Forty unmade, iron grill beds awaited us with a duffel bag standing near each bed. Mine was there but I didn't know which one. A chair stood next to each bed and forty empty lockers lined the walls.

One of the seniors demonstrated the proper technique for making your bed. He flapped the first white flat sheet and covered the entire mattress. The second sheet was the same except he folded it back exactly two inches from the top edge of the mattress. He anchored both sheets with hospital corners and covered them with a heavy brown army blanket. After he snapped a ribbed orange counterpane, he checked that it

77

hung evenly on each side of the bed so that it hid the sheets and the blanket. He tucked one pillow under the counterpane, pounded it flat and smoothed the counterpane so there were no wrinkles. Then he asked, "Any questions?" I had none even though I had never made a bed in my life. I located my duffel bag, unpacked my clothes, stored them in my locker and made my bed best as I could. One of the brothers, a prefect who watched over the dorm, inspected our made beds and reminded us there was to be no talking. We were to keep the "rule of silence." I was never to talk on the top floor of the Juniorate.

After we made our beds, one of the seniors known as our "guardian angel" escorted me around the Juniorate. My angel was Bernard Quigley, a tall boy with bushy black hair who would explain everything I needed to know. I liked Bernard although we differed. He was tall; I was short. He spoke quietly; I had already acquired a reputation of being a loud mouth.

We stopped first at the showers stalls in the middle of the third floor. "Always wear your bathrobe," he instructed. "Never walk from the dormitory to the shower with only a towel around your waist." This would violate the "rule of modesty." So soon two rules—silence and modesty; countless others followed that I would embrace with fervor. The immediate priority of the brothers was to mold me into acting like a pious person. My personal goal was to "strive for perfection," an aspiration impossible to attain but my virtue would be in my striving. I truly thought I could attain perfection.

Next, Bernard showed me the laundry room, with its two by two foot cubicles attached to the walls from floor to ceiling. In the center of the room I saw three laundry bins: one labeled "whites," a second for "colors," and a third "towels." Bernard pointed to a list of names thumb tacked on the wall. Next to my name was the number "6." Each time, before I threw my dirty clothes in the appropriate laundry bin, I'd use an indelible pen to mark the item with my number, "PN6," where the "PN" stood for "Preparatory Novitiate," the official name of the Juniorate. I marked the inside collar of my T-shirts, the inside waist band of the undershorts, and the manufacturer's labels on my desk shirts. I marked "PN6" on the corner of my towels and face cloths. My cubby hole was the third from the bottom and at four feet ten inches I had to stand on the tips of my toes to reach into the back part. In the bin I saw two four inch long safety pins imprinted with the number "6." I didn't need to mark my socks but instead would thread them on the safety pins before throwing them in the appropriate bin.

After Bernard explained the laundry routine, we went down to the second floor where he led me to my desk in the common room, a large study hall with fifteen rows of ten seats, one hundred fifty identical wooden desks. If I forgot which desk was mine I could consult the seating chart at the door. Our next stop was the "small chapel," so called to be distinguished from the "large chapel." Hardly anyone knew its official name, the Chapel of the Divine Childhood. He pointed out his pew and my place next to him and explained how to use the small black prayer book called the "Exercises of Piety" for morning, noon and night prayer. He suggested I say a quick prayer.

The easiest prayer to pray is one of thanksgiving and that's what I prayed. I experienced an immense happiness about just being there.

The last stop on the tour was the refectory, the dining room on the first floor directly under the common room. The sixteen tables with eight places each were already set for our first meal.

As for the other places in the Juniorate, the classrooms, workshops, gymnasiums, music rooms, barber shop, chemistry and physics lab, sports equipment room, shoeshine room, libraries, kitchen and scullery—these would be explained as the need arose. For the first several days I would just follow Bernard around.

I lived life in the Juniorate by the sports seasons. That summer I participated in the "minor" baseball league on the south diamond. The more talented athletes played in the "major" league on the north diamond. When autumn arrived we took calisthenics every afternoon (jumping jacks, touching toes and push-ups) until Brother Bernard deemed our bodies suitably supple for football. When winter arrived we played basketball and when the pond on the eastern end of the property froze, Brother Peter, the Director of the Juniorate, cancelled classes and we played ice hockey most of the day. In early spring I ran cross country and when spring and summer returned it was back to baseball. I thought I lived in a sports academy or a prep school.

But I didn't. The morning bell rang exactly at twenty to six and we had a half-hour to shower, wash, make our bed and report to the small chapel. Morning prayers followed. I used the exercise book to follow the prayers as they were read aloud but the older boys had long since memorized them. After the prayers we sat and Brother Peter would read a scriptural passage. A period of silence followed when everyone engaged in meditation. During the summer we took a course in mental prayer: its methods and its history. I never quite got the hang of it. Instead, as I tried to shut out all worldly thoughts I would inadvertently nod my head and fall asleep. To counter this I was allowed to stand in the pew since it's hard to sleep standing up. I was not alone. On many mornings many heads bobbed during Morning Prayer.

At 6:25 I grabbed my sports jacket from my hook in the alcove outside the small chapel, walked silently through the common room and down a tiny corridor that led to a side door in the front of the large chapel to attend mass. The novices and ancients, all dressed in black robes were already seated in the back. One brother, Brother Cleophas of Mary, an ancient probably in his seventies, who I first considered a maverick, didn't wear his religious habit. His flannel shirt and gray pants desperately needed washing. The buttons on the shirt were long lost and he kept the shirt closed with several safety pins. He never wore shoes, always slippers whose backs were entirely flattened. His right shoulder and arm had been paralyzed and when he limped up to the communion rail with the aid of a cane in his left hand, his right hand swung like a pendulum. At the altar rail where everyone knelt to receive Holy Communion, he stood; kneeling with his crippled legs was impossible.

Brother Cleophas enjoyed his hobby as a ham radio operator. He set up his transmission equipment on a table in an unused alcove of the biology lab on the bottom floor of the Juniorate. The boys in the Juniorate were forbidden to associate with the ancients but in my junior year I would do him a favor and his words of caution would save my life.

Chapter 7

During my years in the Juniorate I reflected on my motives for becoming a brother. They centered on being a teacher and, while my high school environment in the Juniorate resembled the life of a cloistered monk, my future would be back "out in the world" away from the ascetic milieu of a hermitage.

The founder of the Brothers of the Christian Schools, St. John Baptist de La Salle, insisted the brothers would never become clerics. We would be called "brother," not "father." We would take vows; we would not be ordained. As the joke has it, we would not take Holy Orders—a sacrament—but with our vow of obedience we would take orders. Our religious life would center us in a community of confreres.

In 1705 La Salle wrote the rule, a series of statements that guided the brothers. The second article stated that "They [The Brothers] cannot be priests or aspire to the ecclesiastical state, or even sing, wear a surplice, or exercise any function in the church." [5]

At first, La Salle, a priest in the diocese of Rheims, had considered that priests might be members of the order, similar to the structure of the Benedictines and Dominicans whose members are either priests or brothers. He arranged for one of the brothers, Henry L'Heureux, to prepare for the priesthood. Suddenly in 1690 Brother Henry died, and La Salle interpreted his death as a sign from God that the order should not include priests. Thus was born the sole purpose of a vocation to the Christian Brothers—to be a teacher.

Academics in the Juniorate meant serious business for us future teachers. The brothers insisted that everyone attained a four year college degree in an academic subject—majoring in education was unheard of—and so I began the rigorous life of a scholar.

Each brother on the faculty deluged us with assignments—they never called it homework, for that might remind us of home—and the study schedule after supper allowed sufficient time to complete the assignments in the evening. Most of those brothers who taught me in the Juniorate from the summer of 1956 until I graduated in June 1959 included some of the best teachers I have ever had. Few knew as much as they did; they loved what they taught, they loved to teach and few taught more energetically.

When I graduated from St. John's in June 1955, my academic rank had improved from seventeenth in a class of fifty-one to fifth. At St. John's I achieved the status of the proverbial big fish in a small pond. During the year I attended the Day Juniorate I discovered many of the boys were much more intelligent than I. When I arrived in the Juniorate that Sunday June afternoon and walked up that half mile on Station Hill Road, the other boys who walked beside me possessed a lot more smarts than I did. I soon regarded many of them as geniuses; I wasn't wrong. A couple of them became Rhodes Scholars. Learning came naturally to them; their brains acted as academic sponges; they absorbed whatever they were taught. I watched them in class asking questions to clarify a point; when I asked a question I admitted that I didn't really understand the point.

That first summer I took two classes: one in religion and the other in "touch typing." Every weekday morning I reported to the unused biology lab, sat at a desk and stared at a black Underwood typewriter. All the keys had been capped with blanks so I couldn't see the letters and had to refer to a large chart hanging in the front of the room. Brother Robert, who we tagged with the nickname "Typing Bob," walked around the room with a wooden pointer and tapped rhythmically on our desks as he recited the typing exercises. "A-s-d-f-g-space. A-s-d-f-g-space." After the fifth group of letters he'd say "Return"—it sounded like Amen—and almost in unison the thirty-one of us would snap the carriage return of the typewriter back to the left hand margin and continue with the next exercise: "q-w-e-r-t-y-space."

By the beginning of the first semester of my sophomore year, having being drilled daily by Typing Bob, I had mastered touch typing to the tune of forty words per minute. I would spend many hours in the back of the biology lab typing essays, papers, and reports for classes that fall; the brothers discouraged handwritten submissions other than in-class tests.

My courses in the sophomore year included Religion, Latin II, French I, American History, Plane Geometry, and English. I took four courses in the morning from nine to noon, each forty minutes long with five minutes allotted for the changing of classrooms, followed by midday prayers, recitation of the rosary, lunch at twelve-thirty, manual labor and two more courses until three in the afternoon. I fared moderately. Religion eased by; another year memorizing the Baltimore Catechism peppered with commentary from Brother Gerard. He conducted his class by reading the questions from the catechism and calling on one of us to read the answer. He was a gentle soul, soft spoken, and quite nervous. At the slightest disruption—a boy dropping a pencil, a boisterous cough—he accused us of insubordination and demanded we pay more attention. A rumor circulated that he had been sent to teach in the Juniorate because he had a nervous breakdown while teaching in a high school in Detroit. I could believe it and had we been a devious group of students we might have lifted him in his chair—he always taught sitting down—and carried him around the classroom.

I became easily distracted. I'd stare out the window to the basketball courts and baseball fields, glance at the clock on the wall and calculate the time left before recreation started.

Plane Geometry included more memorization but, unlike Brother Gerard in religion class, Brother Gerald planned ahead to June. Brother Gerard barked his words and paced the classroom aisles like a caged lion. Although in his early 30s, he possessed only a half-dozen strands of white hair on his head.

Passing the New York State Regents Examination in geometry required an exact rendition of one of twenty required theorems. Brother Gerald demanded more; our tests were to be absolutely perfect, verbatim plus, word for word, comma for comma and period for period. He insisted our answers must be exactly as those printed in the textbook. During the weeks before the Regents exam, Brother Gerald quizzed us daily. At the beginning of class he walked into the room and merely announced a number from one to twenty. That was the theorem for the quiz. I tried to guess the theorem for the next day but sometimes—with a devilish laugh—he'd ask us to prove the same one as the day before and I regretted not reviewing my previous quiz.

When he graded the theorems, he assigned a score of either ten points or zero points. Although the Regents scoring allowed partial credit, Brother Gerald dismissed it. For him grades were all or nothing. If even one word in the theorem was missing, Brother Gerald assigned a grade of zero. One day I wrote a perfect theorem but neglected to end the theorem with the letters "Q.E.D." which stood for the Latin phrase "Quod Erat Demonstratum" meaning "that which was to be proved." When he returned the quiz he placed it on my desk, pointed to the omission of the obligatory QED—and laughed in a cackle close to high C. He had underlined my zero score in red. We quickly tagged him with the moniker "Merry Gerry." But, unlike Brother Gerard, he knew how to teach and produce results from standardized testing. Many students feared failing the Geometry Regents but even the lowest grades for our class were in the high 80s. Several students scored perfect grades of one hundred. When the academic year ended, we realized that we had been in the hands of a master teacher. For Brother Gerald, the New York State Regents examinations posed no challenge.

Brother Benilde dedicated our English class to reading the anthology "Immortal Poems of the English Language," and for the entire year we navigated the development of English poetry from Chaucer to Dylan Thomas. For certain poets we made extended stops.

When we arrived at Alexander Pope's time, our class paused and examined "The Rape of the Lock" in minute detail. We spent an entire week on this one poem. In my copy of the poetry anthology I wrote voluminous notes explicating the meaning of words like "lap-dogs" and "nymphs," who the Sylphs were, and that ochre was a common card game in the eighteenth century. Another comment I wrote in the margin states that Pope stood only four feet six inches tall. Brother Benilde James taught with that level of detail. I liked this poem of Pope's, if only for the title, which suggested a nastier world existed that I didn't know about. Rape wasn't an ordinary word I heard in the Bronx.

Brother Benilde had recently graduated from Catholic University with a bachelor's degree in English Literature, but his understanding and love of poetic language and the poets suggested to me he had a Ph.D. Besides scrutinizing poems, we read Shakespeare's plays, especially Hamlet, and he demanded we memorize several of the soliloquies and in class deliver them without notes. Brother Benilde deemed the play Hamlet so important that one day he announced that we would be allowed to see a production of the play on television.

He hastily installed a television set in the physics lab but the show on live TV would be broadcast past our bedtime.[6] I am not sure of the exact date but I remember that night.

"Lights out" always occurred at 9 P.M. so the Brother Director granted a dispensation for our class to stay up late. After night prayer, but before the broadcast started, we went to the dormitory, put on our pajamas, slipped on our bathrobes and slippers, and reported to the physics lab. We sat on tall iron stools with no backs, stared at the small black and white television bolted into a corner of the ceiling, and watched the play in silence. In my three years in the Juniorate I watched only that one show on television. After Hamlet ended, we returned to the dormitory to sleep. A discussion of the play would have to wait until the next day in class because we had to keep the rule of Grand Silence that lasted from night prayer until after breakfast the following morning. The experience of altering the nightly routine so we could watch Hamlet on television convinced me of Shakespeare's importance.

I liked English but didn't do very well and found Latin II impossibly hard, so difficult that I had to be tutored by one of the seniors so I could pass. One difficulty I never resolved concerned how to determine the gender of nouns. Why inanimate objects possessed gender baffled me and if I chose the wrong gender I screwed up the case endings when translating.

French I was as bad as Latin I, and French II proved worse. Brother Thomas, who insisted on being addressed as Frère Thomas, had recently returned from studying French in Quebec. At the beginning of each class he gave a quiz, a short English paragraph we had to translate. He scored his ten-point quizzes by subtracting one point for every grammatical error. Often I received a negative score and several times a negative score of two digits because he counted up all the errors and subtracted from ten. When he handed me the test he said, "Uh, Mr. Brennan," and started shaking his finger at me. "So as not to embarrass you, I won't mention your grade out loud. But, in order to pass this course, you've really got to start scoring above zero." I suffered through three years of French and butchered the language daily.

Besides our formal classes, all of us had to join a debating or public speaking team. The Juniorate library subscribed to a magazine "Vital Speeches of the Day" and the brothers encouraged us to read the latest great speeches. Contests were held regularly and we were required to memorize an entire famous speech. For one contest, I chose the speech Robert Emmett, an Irish orator and patriot, delivered to a British court on the eve of his execution in 1803. "Emmett's Speech from the Dock" contained words whose meanings I learned in my English class: predetermination, mitigation, vindication, exculpating, and calumny. If I didn't know the meaning of any of those words, I was expected to figure it out; each one had a Latin root.

The speech sounded like poetry and spilled with alliteration. "Let no man dare when I am dead to charge me with dishonor." I enunciated the "d" words with a flourish and after each one paused briefly. With words and phrases like this I was introduced to the struggles of Irish patriots. I considered my family to be American rather than Irish and knew little about Irish patriots rebelling against British rule. While my father's parents were born in Ireland, my grandmother on my mother's side converted to Catholicism after being raised Episcopalian. Most of my Bronx friends rooted for the Notre Dame football team while I rooted for Navy, the alma mater of my father although he never attended college.

Since Emmet's speech had to be delivered out loud, it had to be practiced out loud. I asked permission during study time in the evening to go to a classroom. I closed the door and pretended I was Robert Emmett on the eve of my own hanging. I was loud to begin with, and other students kidded me about my own private public address system, so raising my voice gave me a good deal of satisfaction. I would scream the opening line of the last paragraph of the speech. "My Lords, you are impatient for the sacrifice."

At the contest on May 31, 1957, I finished second. My only reward was a short insert about the contest on the front page of the final edition of the school newspaper that year. I circled my name and sent that issue home to my parents but that speech assured me that I possessed one of the necessary characteristics of being a teacher—I had no fear of speaking in public and had no trouble being heard.

When afternoon classes ended, I dashed up the stairs to the south dorm, changed into my recreation clothes, and headed for the basketball courts. Since I was always the first one out on the courts, I had time to practice my one and two hand set shots alone, but more importantly, I took hundreds of layups using my left hand. I remembered my father, an unconverted lefthander, and the night when I learned the importance of being able to shoot a basketball with both hands.

I was in the eighth grade, the spring of 1955. It was either a Friday or Saturday night; my father had two tickets to a New York Knicks game. Their opponents were the Boston Celtics led by Bob Cousy, then in his heyday. My father and I took the subway to the old Madison Square Garden on 8th Avenue and 50th Street.

New York City in daylight is not the same New York City at night. And New York City at night near the Madison Square Garden of my childhood is even further removed from reality. Time is suspended. Watching the Knicks play the Celtics at Madison Square Garden was the closest I felt to being in the eternal present.

After we got off the subway, we walked up the exit stairway to the southeast corner of 49th Street and 8th Avenue. The towering Garden was at our backs. The fans, mostly men in wide brimmed hats, spilled out of bars drinking beer out of bottles: Ballantine, Shaefer, and Rheingold: chain smoked non-filtered cigarettes, Chesterfields, just like my father, or puffed on White Owl cigars. Inside, smoke engulfed the

Garden rafters in a gray haze. There were no empty seats and the only snippet of conversation I heard was; "Whaddya think of Cuz?"

The Celtics in the early 1950s, led by Bob Cousy, dominated professional basketball. That night I was not disappointed. At one moment in the game Cousy stole the ball, crossed over the half court line, looked to his left, cut to his right and, dribbling behind his back, laid it up with his right hand. I had only seen this legendary razzle-dazzle move in still photographs in the newspapers my father brought home after driving a bus all day. Watching it live was exhilarating. Moments later, Cousy stole the ball a second time and I remember the anticipatory thrill I had that I would witness the patented move again—twice in one game. Just when I, and most of the fans, thought he would continue to his right, he cut back across the court and laid the ball up with his left hand. Great players changed the game; Cousy could shoot with both hands. Cousy changed the game of basketball; I resolved to imitate his moves.

Cousy was small, only six feet one inch tall, in a game dominated even in 1955 by big men. I was tiny. In my sophomore year in the Juniorate I had barely reached five feet. Cousy was fast. I could run, but Cousy could shoot with both hands; I couldn't. Cousy had learned to do it as a kid when he fell out of a tree and broke his right arm. For years, I would pin my right arm behind my back and practice left handed layups.

I don't think I ever thanked my father for taking me to that game or even for the bus drive with the Washington Senators. When they tore down Madison Square Garden in 1967 and relocated it to its present location at 7th Avenue and 33rd Street, a night in my childhood disappeared with the dust. My mother never thought to give me a camera that evening so I could take a photograph. Jim Harrison, the poet, notes in his poem *Larson's Holstein's Bull* that "Death steals everything except our stories." I have only the memory but I keep trying to tell the stories.

In January 1995 I realized that Boston Garden, whose original name was Boston Madison Square Garden, home of the Celtics, would soon be razed; the parquet floor where Cousy reigned would pass unceremoniously into basketball history. Another memory needed to be made.

My son Mark, like me, is a sports fanatic and I wanted him to be able to say that he saw an NBA basketball game at the original Boston Garden. I bought two tickets to the Saturday, February 18th game and drove to Boston, Massachusetts with Mark. He was fourteen, a little bit older than I was when my father took me. That evening both of us watched the Utah Jazz obliterate the Celtics. John Stockton and Karl Malone ran the back-door play on inept Celtics so often it bored us. That year the Celtics would win the hapless team award but I really wasn't going to see them; I wanted my son to see a location, a Mecca, a shrine of sports basketball. The following September Boston Garden closed and it was demolished two years later. That night in February 1995 the Celtics lost but I won—I consciously created a memory.

Chapter 8

Academics occupied much of my day in the fall of 1956 but the Brothers also inculcated me into a spiritual life. The schedule in the Juniorate resembled a contemplative monastery. Our daily schedule, although abbreviated, followed the canonical hours of the monastic orders.

Our morning prayer resembled the major hours of Matins and Lauds. Monks recited traditional psalms prior to dawn in a simple Gregorian chant melody. On Sundays and the feast days of the major saints we sang Vespers and Compline in the traditional Latin chant. Recitation of the rosary daily, a common Roman Catholic prayer consisting of Our Fathers and Hail Marys, and our midday prayers replaced the recitation of the psalms at Prime, Terce, Sext and None.

At 5:40 A.M. the electric bell on the dormitory wall rang relentlessly for about two minutes and I found it hard to sleep through the noise, although some mornings, exhausted, I never heard it. The Brother Prefect, the proctor for the dorm, paced the aisles tapping a pencil on the steel bed footer to make sure I got out of bed. I felt guilty that this inability to awake instantly revealed my "weakness of the flesh" and I endeavored to overcome it.

The first bell for Morning Prayer rang at 6:25 A.M. If I scurried into the small chapel and slid into my pew as the second bell chimed at 6:30, I indicated my lack of punctuality—another fault to cure. The objective of the spiritual life was "to strive for perfection" and "weakness of the flesh" and "lack of punctuality" were two of the many obstacles I would have to conquer.

While cloistered contemplatives, like the Carthusians or Cisterians of Strict Observance (The Trappists) recited the complete Book of Psalms over the course of a liturgical year, at Morning Prayer, I recited a variety of common prayers and ordinary hymns. The brothers never considered themselves part of the clergy; we were a lay order. I often explained to people who weren't acquainted with the hierarchy of the Roman Catholic Church that a brother was the equivalent of a "male nun." I was not a priest. Our communal prayers differed from the clerical orders and resembled those any ordinary Catholic might pray: the Our Father, the Hail Mary, a variety of petitions to St. Joseph, our guardian angel and the Blessed Virgin to assist us in our daily examination of conscience. During Morning Prayer I reflected intensely on my shortcomings of the previous day.

I stood or knelt during all these recitations and when they were completed I could sit in the pew. After reciting Morning Prayer the Brother Director read a passage from either scripture or one of the Fathers of the Church that complemented the liturgy of the day. Then I tried to engage my mind in mental prayer, a form of meditation, and planned on how to incorporate this scriptural or religious passage into my daily life. If the passage dealt with accepting "the will of God in all things" this might apply to a poor test grade in French class. If it was about "mortification of the flesh" I might not put butter on my toast or salt on my eggs at breakfast; I might even pass on the eggs.

Prayer and meditation introduced new words and phrases into my vocabulary: quietude, active silence, affective prayer and the theory that, if I prayed correctly, my meditation would deepen and I would be joined in a union with God. I should dismiss and banish from my mind all distracting thoughts like how I was going to pass a Latin test later that morning.

At 6:30 we joined the ancient brothers and the newest brothers, the novices, in the large chapel for the celebration of daily Low Mass, a mass that did not include singing. One of the two priests stationed at Sacred Heart Church, the local parish in Barrytown, celebrated the Mass. On most days, Father Dobransky, a young black-haired priest, celebrated in a style that pleased the Brothers: articulate and respectful. On Sundays and major feasts he would celebrate a High Mass where we sang, rather than recited, the prayers.

The Brothers appreciated Father Dobransky's recitation and singing of the Gregorian chant.

On some mornings, however, Monsignor Carroll celebrated mass. He was the pastor of Sacred Heart, a man in his middle sixties, and a curmudgeon at heart. We attributed his grouchiness to an early rising. He would often arrive late and when he hurried up the side aisle toward the sacristy everyone turned tense, especially Brother Gabriel, the Director of Novices, who despised Monsignor Carroll's approach to saying mass. Normally, the recitation of the Gloria would take about two minutes. "Pop" Carroll, as he was called by us in the Juniorate, recited the first words of the Gloria, *Gloria in Excelsis Deo*, then mumbled something and quickly recited the last words of the Gloria, *Dei Patris*. We could do nothing but respond *Amen* and the abridged version of the Gloria would have taken about three seconds. He abbreviated every other prayer: the Credo, the Sanctus, and the Agnus Dei. He raced through the epistle and gospel, cut short the Collect readings, slowed down slightly when he had to genuflect— he may have been arthritic—and the only reason the mass lasted five minutes at all was because he had to distribute Holy Communion to everyone.

After mass we ate breakfast in silence in the refectory. Most religious orders had developed a series of hand signals to communicate at meals so we wouldn't have to speak aloud. Rubbing your thumb against your fingers meant to pass the salt and pepper shakers, pointing your finger and wiggling your thumb like you were shooting a gun meant pass the meat platter and making a fist and rotating it meant pass the milk pitcher. There were at least a dozen others for the vegetable bowl, soup bowl, bread basket, dessert tray and silverware.

While we ate we listened to a boy read on the public address system. First he read a brief biography of the saint of the day from *Butler's Lives of the Saints*, then a scriptural passage for the day and then a chapter from a novel selected by the Brother Director. Some of these novels I found interesting: famous American ones like *Death Comes for the Archbishop* by Willa Cather, obscure American novels like *The Silver Chalice* by Thomas Costain and those novels with special connections to the Brothers like *The Last Hurrah* by Edwin O'Connor who graduated from La Salle Academy, a Brothers' school in Providence, Rhode Island.

At the conclusion of the meal the Great Silence ended and it was permissible to talk but only for a good reason. Morning manual labor followed breakfast. Some boys remained in the refectory clearing and setting the tables for lunch while I scurried around the building cleaning lavatories, mopping floors and dusting every nook and cranny. I envied those boys who received training in cutting hair, painting, plumbing and carpentry; I thought their manual labor more important than mine. Classes started at nine o'clock. Sometimes we hoped that Pop Carroll celebrated mass so we'd get an extra fifteen or twenty minutes before classes to finish any uncompleted school assignments.

For the next three years I repeated this routine every morning. Praying and other exercises of piety continued throughout the day. At noon, after morning classes, we recited midday prayers followed by lunch, more manual labor and afternoon classes until three o'clock. After classes I raced up to the dormitory, changed into my recreation clothes and two minutes later I started shooting hoops on the basketball courts. I was always the first one and running up and down provided relief from the intensity of study and prayer.

At four o'clock I wolfed down a peanut butter and jelly sandwich accompanied by a sugary drink we called "bug juice" and returned to our sports games until 4:20. At five o'clock spiritual reading started in the common room and I read for the next half-hour.

Popular books included *Transformation in Christ* by Dietrich Von Hildebrand, *The Lord* by Romano Guardini and *The Life of Man with God* by Thomas Verner Moore. I received a small brown leather book entitled "Spiritual Notes" and took its title seriously. The first several pages contained guidelines for insuring "the best possible spirit in the Juniorate." I can remember many spiritual lectures where Brother Director emphasized two of those precepts: work on maintaining silence and don't rationalize which meant don't spout excuses when I broke any rules.

I wrote copious notes from my readings and validated them with references to the epistles of St. Paul. I cross checked quotations from the Old Testament. The only blank page in my spiritual notebook is the last one. Some entries are charming; "Saints are just sinners edited and revised." Many entries are quotations; I read a lot of G.K. Chesterton and liked the way he wrote pithy sayings. One entry in particular stands out that would become a mantra for me in times of trouble, "This too shall pass."

Evening prayers followed at 5:30 then dinner, more manual labor, study in the common room, then night prayers and finally bed. There was no such thing as free time. The proverb underlying this regimen that the brothers followed was that "an idle mind is the devil's workshop."

Besides the daily routine of prayer and meditation the Brothers introduced me to another practice that affected my spiritual life. Personal development included having a spiritual director, a person who would guide people to greater spirituality.

I spent the end of each day at my desk in the common room studying and doing assignments. It wasn't called homework since that would remind me of home and that wasn't a good thought to have. I had left my family, that wasn't hard for me; I didn't miss them but other boys disliked being away from their family. They were lonely, homesick and when the Brother Director met with them he assisted them to maintain their vocation and overcome the desire to return home or, conversely, convinced them to return home. The Brother Director could see that for some boys the rigors of living a semi-cloistered life proved too austere and too demanding.

One method of encouraging this development of the spiritual life involved a weekly meeting with the Brother Director called "reddition." Many English dictionaries do not include the word. The Oxford English dictionary only defines an archaic meaning, to surrender or give back. The word meant something quite different in the Juniorate.

Once a week, at an assigned time, I met with the Brother Director. We called this meeting weekly our reddition. I stood at his office door waiting for the previous boy to come out, then I entered and told the Brother Director what kind of difficulties I might be having. It was like an informal confession; tell the Brother Director your shortcomings but not your sins.

The Brother Director already knew how I felt about my family and how they felt about me. Every Sunday morning I had to write a letter to my parents. I dropped these letters unsealed into a wire bin on one of the empty desks at the rear of the common room and every letter was read by the Brother Director before it was sealed and mailed to my parents. My mother wrote letters. My father wrote notes accompanied by newspaper clippings of baseball box scores. These letters my parents sent were already slit open when they were delivered to my desk. I wondered if the Brother Director actually read all these letters and one day I discovered he did. During one reddition he asked me to do him a favor. He selected a letter from the pile on his desk. It was the latest letter from my father. "Your father's handwriting is impossible to read," he said. "Can you ask him to write more clearly?"

When I wrote my next letter I told my father I found his left handed handwriting illegible. After that my father sent only typewritten letters.

I felt uncomfortable during reddition. We rarely talked about feelings and emotions in my family and I constantly tried to find topics to talk about that would carry me through the fifteen minute session. I worried a lot about my grades, wondering how I might improve so I talked about them. My concern about poor grades didn't seem to worry the Brother Director. God will provide was the general attitude in case there wasn't any human solution. Since all the brothers who taught us lived together and talked about us, if I was really in academic trouble, they would find a solution and they did. During my sophomore year my Latin grades deteriorated from bad to atrocious so that during nightly study in the common room the Brother Director granted permission for me to go to a classroom where one of the seniors, so accomplished that he could carry on conversations in Latin, tutored me. I could hardly conjugate a regular verb much less an irregular one and could never divine why some nouns were masculine and others feminine.

But the Brother Director's interest concerned my psychological state. When he asked me if I had any thoughts about returning home I could answer emphatically that I did not. Other boys didn't want to stay. They couldn't overcome their homesickness. Our derogatory word for those who left the Juniorate was that they "fluked" with the implication that they weren't mentally tough enough. It didn't bother me at all that I was separated from my family at such an early age.

We all knew immediately when someone fluked because he didn't arrive in chapel for Morning Prayer. A boy, about to fluke, never told anyone—at least no one ever told me. After everyone left the dorm for Morning Prayer he returned and packed his belongings. While we prayed he ate breakfast and the Brother Director drove him to the train station for the trip back to Grand Central Terminal.

Brother Thomas, a moderately absent-minded man who taught French, seemed to miss these events when someone fluked. One morning, at the start of French class, he took attendance and came to the name of a boy who had returned home that morning. "Levandowski?" he called. Silence. He repeated it again. "Levandowsk? Chester Levandowski?" He scanned the room thinking Chester had not heard him. Finally, someone spoke in a serious voice, "Chester is no longer with us." It sounded like he had died.

Another spiritual practice in the Juniorate to deepen my spiritual life was an adaptation of a monastic tradition, when monks confessed aloud their own faults to the abbot in the presence of the other monks in order to acquire the virtue of humility. In many Roman Catholic religious orders the practice is called the "Chapter of Faults." St. La Salle modified it and called it "Advertisement of Defects" where, instead of proclaiming your own faults, others, ostensibly motivated by charity, would accuse you. In the Juniorate the weekly ritual was called "Shots" as in being "shot at with a pistol." My notebook "Spiritual Notes" contains an entry; "There is no humility without humiliation." On Thursday evenings I would be humiliated with an abundance of shots.

At the end of our study time, just before night prayer, the Brother Director walked to the front of the common room, took his seat behind a large desk on a raised dais and gaveled us to order. I removed all my books, notes, pens and pencils and stored them inside my desk. My desktop was cleared so I would have no distractions. I clasped my hands as if I was praying; actually I was praying that the mortification this week wouldn't be as bad as last week.

When the Brother Director gaveled again, the boy in the first seat in the first row stood up and recited the following prayer aloud. "My very dear Brothers, I beseech you to have the charity to advertise me of my defects, so that, knowing them I may correct myself with the grace of God." Then the boy just stood there waiting like a bulls-eye poster to be shot. Anyone could stand up and accuse him of whatever fault he had, real or imagined, trivial or serious, true or untrue. While the prayer the boy recited requested charity, precious little of it was delivered. The weekly exercise served only to be mortified, insulted and disgraced. Those seated in the front of the room had the disadvantage of not be able to see their accusers, who they were or even how many were standing attentively waiting their turn to accuse. If I was unfortunate enough to have a seat in the front of the common room then when it was my turn to stand and be accused I tried to identify the person by voice so that when it was his turn to be advised of his faults I could return the humiliation in kind if not worse. When accused I had no defense; I could not refute; I could not turn and say "that is not true." I maintained silence as the accusations accumulated like falling snow. When the Brother Director gaveled again I recited another prayer thanking my accusers, the most insincere prayer I have ever prayed. Physically weak with embarrassment, I often sat down at my desk shaking, wondering how I could have so many defects. I could hardly remember them all. It would be a long time before I would overcome this feeling of futility and inadequacy. If any egotists lived among us they would be shattered like a hammer hitting pottery.

The accusers recited the offense by saying, "It seems to me my very dear brother that" and then the details followed. Many accusations were trivial. "It seems to me my very dear brother your genuflections are sloppy." Or "you eat your food too quickly." Or "you brush your hair too vainly." Granted, others accusations were more substantive about my argumentative behavior and loud voice: "You get too hotheaded during basketball games," "You quarrel and yell at the referees too much," and "You take sports too seriously." I must admit some of these were true but they weren't faults. Hotheadedness was really passion for the game, referees were usually blind and I always took sports seriously. I probably learned this from my father. Had he not arranged a legal hooky day for me from St. John's to ride with Washington Senators?

There was one accusation, however, that struck deeply at my psychological state. The Juniorate housed nearly one hundred boys, ages fifteen to eighteen, maturation years where attraction to the opposite sex blossomed if only in our imaginations. But there were no girls to be attracted to—only boys, and the faculty feared of the absence of girls might encourage homosexual tendencies. While friendships were allowed exclusive friendships were not. Any personal expression of affection of one boy to another, touching another boy on the hand or the arm, hugging or embracing was strictly forbidden and would not be tolerated. The religious mores discouraged hanging around with only one another person; groups were safer, the larger the better. Pairing off with another boy, walking in twos after supper at night, or even talking sports one-on-one on the ball field in order to develop a friendship, was explicitly banned. If this kind of deleterious relationship existed it was referred to as a "particular friendship," a "PF" as we called it, and I was not to form one under any circumstances nor let one be formed with me. The most dreaded accusation during advertisement of defects was "It seems to me my very dear brother that you are developing a particular friendship." Fortunately, the object of one's affection was never named but everyone knew who it was and if the relationship continued it would be cause for expulsion. The expression used, in this circumstance, was that if you didn't shape up you'd be "shipped" out. When a boy was shipped out and sent home the Brother Director worked the following scriptural passage from the Gospel of St. Matthew 20:16 into his spiritual lectures. I, like all the others who remained, had been called but he reminded us that while "many are called few were chosen."

The most popular faculty members in these early years of formation were the Brothers

Sub-Directors. We appreciated them not for what they did but what they didn't do.

When the Brother Director was absent on Thursday evenings and unable to conduct the ritual of "Shots" he delegated the responsibility to the Brother Sub-Director. Most of them would have none of it; they had experienced it. No sooner had a boy started the prayer inviting his defects to be announced when Brother Sub-Director gaveled the boy silent and indicated he should immediately recite the ending prayer. He gaveled each of us like a metronome so there was no time for anyone to stand and accuse. Each boy hardly had time to recite the entire prayer. An exercise of piety that usually lasted more than a half an hour was over in less than five minutes. We retired immediately to chapel for night prayer. One of the prayers began "Let us thank God for his graces and benefits." On those evenings, reprieved from embarrassment, we recited this prayer louder and with extra enunciation. Our enthusiastic tone and cadence was unmistakable especially at the last line of the prayer. We made sure we emphasized our gratitude by pausing at certain words. "I thank Thee for all the special graces which, in Thy bounty, Thou hast... *this day*... conferred upon me." While the prayer was addressed to God, it was our way of thanking the Brother Sub-Director for sparing us humiliation for at least a week.

Other than reddition and "shots" I remember being quite content and happy, absorbing every religious idea like a sponge. In my three years in the Juniorate it never occurred to me that I might leave and return home.

Chapter 9

Everyone referred to the brothers in the Home Family Community as the "ancients" and while the term signified most of them were physically old, most of us in the Juniorate considered them "the revered" or the venerable brothers. Their professional careers had earned our respect. We had heard stories about their teaching and their lives had inspired us.

They had spent most of their religious lives in a teaching community at a school until their medical demands increased and, their health deteriorating, they came to Barrytown since they need constant care. Some of them left the classroom reluctantly, unable to realize their teaching life had ended. One of them said to me, "I often thought I will die teaching in the front of a classroom. I will fall down and they will pick me up off the floor."

Many of them spoke plainly, relating profound stories with simple words about their forty or fifty years as a teacher. Several had managed a renowned school as its principal: La Salle Academy on 2nd Street in Manhattan; Bishop Loughlin High School in Brooklyn and Lincoln Hall in Lincolndale, New York, a residential school for boys who were one court appearance away from a cell in a New York State prison. Those Brothers who worked at "The Hall" were especially admired for they fulfilled more truly the tradition of St. La Salle that the mission of the Brothers of the Christian Schools was to teach the poor gratuitously. I never heard any brother complain about being assigned to teach at Lincoln Hall. Many brothers requested the assignment and were disappointed when they were denied.

Now, elderly and at different stages of infirmity, the ancients spent their lives in quiet prayer. A few of them relished the chance to be contemplative, to meditate and to pray. They knew Barrytown would be their last assignment. Within a couple of feet, they knew the location of their plot in the cemetery just beyond the cherry trees on the road to the chicken coop.

When an ancient died, the Juniorate schedule changed the next day. Brother Director cancelled many manual labor assignments after breakfast and assigned twice as many boys to refectory and scullery duty so it could be cleaned in half the time. He shortened some classes and at eleven o' clock we returned to the large chapel for a high Requiem Mass followed immediately by interment. Once a week we practiced the sections of Gregorian chant to be sung on the following Sunday. We hardly ever practiced the chant for the Requiem Mass since we sang it often. In

November 1957, three brothers died within ten days of each other.

Every morning at Mass I eyed the Director of the Ancients, Brother Concordius Leo, as he pushed Brother Richard strapped in his wheelchair up the center aisle of the large chapel to the communion rail. To me Brother Leo's example was admirable; he was the Director yet he considered himself the servant. Brother Concordius Leo, we called him Conky, wore a perpetual smile and, if not the kindest, one of the kindest men I ever met.

Brother Richard, ravaged by Parkinson's disease, couldn't control his own body. Despite his head braced against the back of the wheelchair with a white sash across his forehead, his eyes unable to focus and his mouth in a perpetual oval he accepted God's will. His alert mind knew when the priest stepped through the altar railing gate and into the main aisle of the nave to administer Holy Communion and he stuck his tongue out as far as he was able to receive the host. After he received the host he made halting gestures with his right hand that I assumed was an attempt to make the sign of the cross. I thought Brother Richard, and his companions, saints on earth. My others shared my admiration.

Brother Oliver Joseph, known as "Ollie Joe," supervised the vegetable garden with horticultural expertise. Ollie Joe had lived at Barrytown since it opened in 1930 and had managed a garden at the previous novitiate in Pocantico Hills, New York. He kept perpetual silence and legend had it that no one had ever heard him speak.

111

His garden produce included strawberries, rhubarb, onions, potatoes, lettuce, cabbage and kale. In the early summer I welcomed the prestige manual labor assignment in "Ollie Joe's Garden" to pick and pack strawberries. Not every strawberry landed in the quart baskets I dragged along the furrows. I never balked at the stomach ache caused by eating too many ripe strawberries, some the size of a golf ball.

Other assignments, like picking corn on the hardscrabble acres at the far eastern fields near River Road, meant real manual labor. On those afternoons I wore a long sleeve shirt to protect my arms from the rough stalks, a wide brimmed hat for sun protection and I watched for lazy snakes sunning themselves in open patches or ambitious ones searching for field mice. I sweated. I got dirty but I noticed that corn snakes were beautiful in their yellow and tan skins.

None of the ancients had any reason to enter the Juniorate building. The exception was Brother Cleophas of Mary, the brother who shuffled to the communion rail at daily mass. His hobby, operating a ham radio station, required him to limp through the Juniorate refectory, climb up the stairs to the first floor and into the unused biology lab where he stored his equipment in the alcove in the front of the lab.

Our paths met. My expertise with my 35mm camera didn't go unrewarded and I finagled an assignment as an unofficial photographer for *The Beacon*, the school newspaper. I learned how to use a Graflex camera: loading the 4 x 5 sheets of film into the back of the camera, setting the focal lens depending on the reading of a light meter and then developing the film in the tiny photography lab in the corridor next to the biology lab. Depending on the urgency to develop film when the newspaper was going to the printer, or when the Brother Director wanted a print immediately, I was allowed to work in the photo lab while the others recited evening prayer or were engaged in spiritual reading. At the door to the biology lab my photography routine and Brother Cleophas's radio operations crossed.

Late one afternoon during recreation, I took some sport shots of boys playing basketball and then went to the photo lab to develop the film. We both arrived in the corridor leading to the biology lab at the same time. His presence there was nothing unusual and we didn't say anything to each other. Many afternoons I overheard him trying to contact other ham operators by reciting his radio handle as he scanned over several frequencies.

"CQ, CQ, CQ, this is W2HLA," he recited into his microphone. Then he announced a phrase clarifying the call letters of his handle to anyone in the Western Hemisphere who might be listening. "We're two happy little angels" he said. "W2HLA," he repeated.

That afternoon, instead of talking to people around the world, he had trouble trying to install several new vacuum tubes into his power supply. Since one of his arms hung uselessly, he couldn't hold the power supply firmly and at the same time insert the vacuum tubes into the proper slots. As I left the photo lab he saw me and called. I wasn't supposed to engage any of the ancients in conversation but he insisted. His tone of voice indicated that if I didn't help him I would be guilty of being disobedient. The Juniorate policy, when I needed clarification about whether I could do something or not and the Brother Director wasn't immediately available to ask, was to "presume permission" that, if asked, the action would be allowed. I presumed permission to assist Brother Cleophas; I entered the biology lab and approached Brother Cleophas at the table.

First, he asked me to lift up my pant cuffs so he could see my feet. I was wearing my basketball sneakers, white high-top Keds with thick rubber soles. He inspected them for a moment. Satisfied, he emphasized that I keep both my feet and my chair completely on the thick rubber mat that ran along the floor next to the table.

He unpacked the vacuum tubes from their boxes: Philco, RCA and Emerson brands and he pointed to their proper place in the power supply. I reached in, rotated the tubes so the prongs and the sockets matched and secured them firmly but carefully. After inserting one or two tubes I must have gotten careless and touched a wire or a cord that grounded me. I sprang up out of the chair like a jack-in-the-box and landed on the floor. My arm tingled from my finger tips to my shoulder blade with an acute case of pins and needles.

I sat stunned on the rubber mat. I don't know how many volts I had survived but Brother Cleophas, apparently unperturbed, first tapped my sneakers with his cane and then he tapped the rubber mat.

"You're lucky to be alive," he said.
"What happened?" I asked.

He gave me a quick lesson on the relationship of voltage and amperage. I suddenly became more interested in physics.

I never told anyone that I presumed permission to assist Brother Cleophas, nor that I was jolted and Brother Cleophas didn't either but, from that afternoon on, I became his unofficial assistant. Whenever I was around the photo lab I'd glance into the biology lab to see if he needed help. He taught me how to operate the tuner and distinguish human voices amid the static in the speakers. If I made contact with any other ham operator I had to note the call letters, time and date of transmission and the person's location in the world and he logged the information in a black and white marble notebook he kept on the table. Before I operated the ham radio I never knew where Chile was; I learned a lot of geography.

Events in the next several months complemented my relationship with Brother Cleophas. For most of my sophomore and junior years my manual labor assignments were quite manual with much labor. One of my assignments required cleaning the first floor lavatories, one of the lowest level jobs which consisted of swirling a mixture of industrial strength soap around the toilets and urinals, restocking the toilet paper, cleaning the windows and mirrors and mopping the floors. Manual labor assignments rotated every month and I guess I became an expert at urinal detail because when the next round of assignments was announced I continued my duties in the first floor lavatories. My reward came in my senior year with my assignment to the infirmary located in the ancients building. This job allowed me to wander around the building that was otherwise off limits.

The infirmary responsibilities included more lavatory duty but also keeping the infirmary rooms immaculate. Since we lived in such close quarters, germs weaved their way through the Juniorate like falling dominos. During the winter it was routine for many of the infirmary rooms to be occupied with either novices or juniors who had succumbed to the flu. One summer the "Asian flu" as we called it claimed so many Juniors that our summer vacation with our families started a week earlier than usual.

I wasn't allowed to speak with the novices recuperating in the infirmary since they were cloistered but my duties included delivering the necessary books to Juniorate students in the infirmary so that the sick person could complete the assignments for his classes. After a person was discharged from an infirmary room, it needed a complete sanitization: spraying every surface with disinfectant, washing and waxing the floor, and undoing the bed including the mattress cover and bringing the linens to the laundry room in the basement of the ancients building so they could be washed and dried separately from the general laundry. I had the freedom to wander around the ancients building: down to the laundry room or up to an ancient's room third or fourth floor to deliver linens. I usually walked up the rarely used back staircase and discovered the stairs continued directly to the roof.

One morning, when I was sure no one would miss me for a couple of minutes, I climbed to the top landing, opened the door and stepped out onto the tar roof. The 180° panoramic view of the Hudson Valley reminded me of the one from my grandmother's kitchen window but at this height I could see much farther. To the west across the Hudson River stood Round Top, a mountain in the Catskills, where I could make out an abandoned hotel at its summit. To the south, I saw the Kingston Rhinecliff Bridge that had just been completed in the fall of 1956. To the north I could make out buildings in the town of Saugerties, New York.

After the bridge was built, our method of travelling back home during vacations changed. We no longer returned to New York City on the New York Central railroad but on a rented bus that crossed the bridge and connected to the recently completed New York Thruway to the Yonkers border and then to Manhattan College in the Riverdale section of the Bronx. I felt disappointed since I always had an affection for riding on the railroad.

During the senior year I, and four of my closer friends, formed a quintet and performed at assemblies on the major feast days: Halloween (always called All Hallows Eve), Christmas and St. Patrick's Day. We practiced our repertoire in the Juniorate scullery where the acoustics of the high ceilings and tiled walls resembled a gigantic shower stall. When we performed we wore charcoal gray pants, pink shirts and scarlet V-neck sweaters. Our crooning imitated the popular groups of the era and while I was content just to belt out a tune I didn't realize the other members of the group let the lyrics influence them too

much.   We sang *Smoke Gets In Your Eyes* like
The Platters, longed for *Donna* as sung by Ritchie
Valens and could only imagine what Frankie
Avalon's *Venus* was like. I enjoyed the melodies
of the songs; they yearned for the girls on the
Rockaway boardwalk.

Since I worked with Brother Cleophas on
the sly, I had access to radio equipment, mainly
crystal diodes, the main component of construct-it-
yourself AM radios.   Since I worked in the
infirmary and had access to the roof, I planned my
petty thefts. I borrowed enough copper wire from
Brother Cleaphas's supplies, snuck it up to the
roof of the ancients' building, anchored one end to
a bolt on the roof and dropped the rest of the wire
to the ground. From the window in the supply
room in the infirmary, I gathered in the wire,
connected it to a confiscated crystal diode, an AM
tuner, attached them to the antenna and grounded
the entire circuit on a radiator. Since the antenna
was so long not only could I clearly hear the AM
station from Saugerties but, on some occasions,
when I delivered the homework assignments to the
sick later in the evening when radio waves
bounced off the stratosphere more efficiently, I
listened to disk jockey Bruce Morrow (soon to
become Cousin Brucie) or Alan Freed on WINS
and WABC out of New York City and if I heard a
tune our group was practicing I'd try and get the
correct tempo and pass it along to the other
members of my group. It's a wonder the faculty
brothers didn't catch on that I knew all the lyrics
to songs I couldn't possibly have heard.

Toward the end of my senior year in the
spring of 1959 another trio of brothers died in

rapid succession. The first death occurred on February 23, the second on March 4. On the feast of St. Patrick Brother Cleophas of Mary, my ham radio mentor, died after a short illness. It wasn't until several weeks later when I read his obituary in *The Beacon* that I realized he had spent his entire life teaching the underprivileged. The list of his assignments where he took care of the poorest of God's poor sounds like institutions from a Dickens' novel: New York Catholic Protectory, Utica Asylum, Hillside Hall, and a reform school in Halifax, Nova Scotia. Less than a week later, almost all his ham radio equipment disappeared from the biology lab. The room had a hole in it. On a window shelf the cleanup crew had forgotten to remove two vacuum tubes: a Sylvania, model FH, and a Philco, model 35-0-1-123 T with the admonition on its base that "when renewing insist on a genuine Philco tube." They sat there like orphans. I stuck both of them in my pocket and for the next fifty years have used them in my mathematics and computer science classes. When I act out my version of "show and tell" I say they are examples of "ancient" technology but no one really knows what I mean by the word ancient. An ancient was a person. To this day the word ancient, to me, always means a person worthy of respect.

On June 7, 1959 I graduated from the Juniorate with twenty-one others. In the course of three years of high school in the Juniorate about ten people either fluked or were shipped. Three weeks later I packed up my duffel bag once more and loaded it on the truck that drove it around the property a quarter mile to the Novitiate. When the truck was unpacked, I realized that the others members of my singing group were on their way back home. After all our singing together not one of them said goodbye. We had spent so much time together and now they were gone. I guess they were told not to tell me they were leaving, returning to the world; it might have given me second thoughts. For them, a life of celibacy in a fully cloistered Novitiate for the next fourteen months and the rest of their lives wasn't what they were called to. For me, I was anxious to start my real religious life. I quickly forgot them; many others would soon enter my life.

Chapter 10

In the summer of 1959 I crossed over from the Juniorate building to the Novitiate and became a postulant, the formal designation of a person who requests to be accepted into a religious order. The Juniorate provided limited contact with the outside world, but when I entered the Novitiate, I accepted a comprehensive cloistered environment. I wrote few letters home, maybe once a month, and there wasn't much to write about except that I prayed six hours a day, attended a class in church history and another in the history of the Christian Brothers. I read only spiritual or theological books, no literature or poetry; newspapers were forbidden. I gave up my crystal radio set. There was no TV in the novitiate. Most of what happened in the outside world from July 1959 until September 1960 I learned later from history books.

The only magazines allowed dealt with liturgical studies and religious affairs, although Brother Gabriel subscribed to two popular Catholic commentary magazines: *America*, published by the Jesuits, and *Commonweal*. When he finished reading them, he placed them in the magazine rack in the common room. I read some of the articles in these magazines but, with a limited ability to understand political and philosophical writings, could not decipher the importance of events occurring in the outside world. Most of the articles promulgated a Christian, if not Roman Catholic, slant on the world of politics. Many of the authors, the prominent Catholic voices of the time, wrote essays advocating Christianity as a social force: Dorothy Day, the leading proponent of social justice and a pacifist; Francois Mauriac, a French novelist who had won the Nobel Prize for literature in 1952; Daniel Berrigan, a Jesuit priest who took Dorothy Day's pacifism and turned it into a crusade against the war in Vietnam; and Gerard Sloyan, another Jesuit and the foremost American authority about the liturgy of the Catholic Church. Subconsciously, I absorbed all their arguments about how Christianity should be lived in the modern world. Two years later I would be privileged to sit in one of Father Sloyan's classes at the Catholic University of America.

In late June and early July the Novitiate grew more crowded. Though only twenty-one junior novices had decided to enter the Novitiate, more than four dozen postulants who came from "the world," joined us. In early July we numbered more than seventy. Those who joined us had attended the high schools administered by the Brothers. The schools in New York City I knew: La Salle Academy on 2nd Street, Manhattan Prep on the campus of Manhattan College in the Bronx, and St. Peter's High School on Staten Island. Other schools in the district I had only heard about: St. Raphael's in Pawtucket, Rhode Island, St. Mary's in Waltham, Massachusetts, and St. Joseph's in Buffalo, New York. It was the beginning of living with and understanding people different from my own parochial New York City background. At first, there were differences of opinion among us about who would make the best religious, those of us who came from the Juniorate or those who had more experience in the world and understood what they were giving up.

Those of us who had attended the Juniorate acted as if we were superior and that our earlier calling exalted us. I argued frequently with Christopher Kieran who, before he entered the Novitiate, had completed his freshman year at Manhattan College. In a periodic exchange of essays we each claimed our own experience more advantageous for confronting the rigors of the religious life. I defended the concept of a Juniorate and emphasized that during those three years my official status was as a junior *novice*. He claimed that no teenage boy could possibly have the mental or emotional capacity of selecting his life work.

After a month our differences faded. The Novitiate evolved into a community of young men, eighteen and nineteen years old, preparing intensely for a lifetime in a religious order. In the Novitiate I needed to develop and foster a deep spiritual life and, if I did, at the end of the Novitiate I would take five temporary vows for one year: the three traditional ones in Roman

Catholic monastic orders, poverty, chastity, and obedience, and two more vows particular to the Brothers of the Christian schools: stability and teaching the poor gratuitously.

The postulancy lasted through the summer months of July and August. Some postulants withdrew and returned to the world. The rigors proved too tough for them to handle. Our numbers dwindled to less than sixty and finally, during the first week of September, settled at fifty-three.

The traditional date for the official taking of the religious habit occurred on the eve of the feast of the Nativity of the Virgin Mary. On the morning of September 7, 1959, after processing into the chapel from the vestibule, we took our places in the first pews and recited some introductory prayers. Then all the postulants stood. Brother Anthony John, the Brother Visitor, a title similar to the president of an organization, called each of us by our secular name. The invitation to become a member of the order had to be extended through a brother in the order who would sponsor the postulant. When my name was called, I approached the altar rail accompanied by my sponsor, Brother Eugene, who had taught me at St. John's. I genuflected and then bowed to Brother John. He held the habit, I knelt in front of him and extended my arms palms up to accept it. The postulants with their sponsors adjoined to the Juniorate common room. I took off my jacket and tie and white shirt. Then Brother Eugene dressed me in the habit, the simplest of religious garb, a black, shoulder-to-ankle cassock with no embroidery, fastened from waist to neck by tiny black hooks rather than buttons. Unlike those of other monastic orders, the Brothers' habit had no accessories. I wore no cincture around my waist and there was no cowl at the shoulders. Around my neck I wore the rabat, a clerical collar with two broad white extensions that resembled a short starched bib. Just before Brother Eugene slipped the robe over my head I kissed the collar of the habit.

After our robing we reassembled in the large chapel. Several minutes earlier, the young men kneeling in those pews had been a group of individuals dressed in a variety of suit jackets and different colored ties. Now we were a religious community, an assembly of men dressed in identical black habits. The ceremony continued and each new novice received a copy of the Exercises of Piety, a black beaded six decade rosary (one decade more than the traditional rosary), and adopted a new name. I understood that for the rest of my life I would be known by this name; it was my religious name and would for many years be my legal name. I chose a name after a saint that I thought reflected my personality: hard-headed, impetuous and loyal to a fault—Peter. The brothers assigned me a second name. I became Brother Peter Terrance; Thomas Howard Brennan no longer existed. To this day when I see some of my friends, they call me Peter.

My immediate family along with the families of the other postulants sat in the rear of the large chapel. My mother smiled, happy that one of her sons would dedicate himself to God. My father seemed accepting. My sister Jeannie, age thirteen, and my brother Bobby, age eleven, gaped in awe.

At the end of ceremony we processed outside and my parents joined me. My mother snapped many photos and after a light lunch in the novitiate all-purpose room I said my goodbyes and my family returned home. I would not see them again until the following September when I would pronounce first vows.

The Director of Novices, Brother Angelus Gabriel, taught us the procedures for mental prayer: clearing the mind of distractions, asking God for enlightenment and submitting our will to the will of God. Brother Albinus of Mary, the Sub-Director lectured us in the history of the Church and in particular the writings of our founder St. John Baptist de la Salle. I would study the nature of contemplative prayer, the writing of the Fathers of the Church, and the history of the Brothers like any other academic subject except there would be neither tests nor grades.

I wrote in my novitiate spiritual journal about the three stages of contemplation: "multiple reflections, few reflections and simple attention." I had difficulty advancing from the first state of contemplation. My mind always had multiple reflections. I found it impossible to concentrate on only one idea. No matter what the topic (God, sin, heaven, hell, virtue, suffering, penance), I could never anchor the idea long enough to meditate on it. It evaporated before I had time to understand its importance. I could never quick freeze my mind into a state of contemplation.

I worried about this shortcoming, concluding I was incapable of contemplation, until

I realized that everyone else had the same problem. In the novitiate I arose at five in the morning, almost an hour earlier than in the Juniorate. In the winter, in order to wake up, I donned a coat and briskly walked several laps around the oval in front of the large chapel. Morning prayers began at 5:30, followed by a reading from the Brother Gabriel, the Director of novices, and then I attempted to meditate on that reading until Mass started at 6:30.

For some, staying awake in the chapel proved impossible, even in the winter when we could see our breath float to the top of the chapel as we exhaled since the hissing radiators hadn't yet warmed the vast space of the nave. Standing was permitted, but not sitting, and if a novice remained kneeling, on many mornings he fell asleep. This wasn't the mere nodding of the head as occurred in the Juniorate. This was complete slumber. First, the body would relax, the shoulders would droop and the clasped hands held over the front of pew would loosen. Then the head would bob and finally, when sleep arrived, the entire head would jerk in a spasm, jolting the person awake, and the process would start again. Sometimes the spasm of waking abruptly caused the novice to fall off his kneeler.

One theme of the Brother Director's morning lectures explained the vows I would take at the end of the year. The essence of the vow of poverty pushes communism to its logical conclusion; a novice did not own anything personally. All property belonged to the community. My parents stopped sending forty dollars a month for my education and board. I had the three necessities of life: food, shelter and clothing. If I needed a new pair of pants, I submitted a request. If I needed a new pencil, I submitted a request. We wrote our names only on notebooks and personal spiritual journals. No one else ever read these. My accounting of my spiritual life—how humble I was, how I detached myself from material things, how patiently I acted—these pious characteristics and their development existed between myself and God.

Poverty, the word, is usually understood as being poor and having little money and no wealth. Poverty, the vow, meant that I could share in whatever wealth the institute or community enjoyed. Money, as a means of commodity interchange, didn't exist. During my entire three years in the Juniorate and the year in the Novitiate I never handled money. No monetary system existed and money was worthless, but I was never poor.

I remember one incident in the Juniorate in the summer between my junior and senior year. It was June 21, 1958. The school year had ended and to keep us busy before summer school started Brother Benilde organized a day-long hike. We started by walking the trails that led through the farm section of the property and into the woods that bordered the Hudson River. Our route bypassed the Bard College campus and hooked up to Cruger Island Road and then we walked west along the road to the Hudson River. It was hot and buggy and soon we reached a stream that flowed into the Hudson River. The water was cold but refreshing and the rocky terrain created wading pools. Acting impulsively, I decided to cool off. I slipped off my sneakers and rolled my pants up above my knees and stepped into the water. The black water soon started to turn slightly red and I wondered if I had stirred up some silt at the bottom of the stream. When I went back to the shore line to put on my sneakers I realized I had stepped on something razor sharp but I had felt no pain. A quarter of my right heel hung off my foot. I used my sock to press my heel together but the amount of blood turned my sock red. Soon I was sprawled face up on the grass and Roger Bracken and several boys wrapped my foot with a sweat shirt and more socks in order to stem the bleeding. It was impossible for me to walk much less hike through the woods back to the Juniorate so a half a dozen junior novices hoisted me to their shoulders and carried me to the nearest road. Two of the other junior novices ran back to the Juniorate alerting another brother who drove out and picked me up. Rather than go back to the infirmary he drove me directly to the emergency room at Rhinebeck Hospital where my heel was stitched back together. The doctors voiced concern that I would develop an infection and I heard murmurs about amputation. I remained in the hospital for observation for two days and recovered.

My mother made that occasion the last entry in my baby book. She wrote, "At Barrytown, N.Y. Cut foot at heel wading in stream. Rhinebeck Hospital 2½ days. 9 stitches." I guess my mother felt that, even at the age of 17, I was still her baby. Only much later did I ask the question, "Who paid the hospital bill?" It was the Brothers. In fact, I don't believe they ever informed my parents of the accident. In my next letter home I related the incident, downplaying its importance by writing that "I got my first stitch when I cut myself on my foot." I remember trying hard to figure out how to avoid saying I had nine stitches. My mother, not fooled by my ruse, probably called the Brother Director.

I wasn't reprimanded but the incident cemented my reputation that there were few ordinary events that I could not turn into trouble. After I left the hospital on crutches I realized I had created my own punishment; rather than play baseball that summer I merely watched.

Chapter 11

Unlike the Juniorate, the Novitiate proved grueling in its predictability of prayer followed by more prayer with hardly a diversion in the daily schedule. One by one our numbers dwindled and, for the first time in four years, I questioned whether I had a vocation.

Brother Gabriel, the Director of Novices, knew he could never attain perfection. He had one bad, unbreakable habit. He always talked in a whisper and never looked directly at me when conversing. When he spoke privately in his office, I had to slide to the edge of my chair and lean my head toward him to catch all his words. His entire body exuded shyness and his face, tinged a perpetual red, gave the impression he was always blushing. While he talked he stared at his hands and rubbed the four fingers of his right hand in and against the four fingers of his left hand as if he was trying to cradle an egg. I stared at his hands and saw the one fault he couldn't overcome. The tips of his fingers on his right hand shone like saffron—Brother Gabriel chain smoked.

He tried to conceal it but we lived close together in the novitiate and I observed him as much as he observed me. Since he couldn't smoke inside the building, he took his morning stroll in the woods. After breakfast, when all the novices reported to their morning manual labor assignment, Brother Gabriel retired to his room, took off his habit and put on a sweat shirt. He exited the Novitiate building by the back door, hurried across the road past the outdoor Stations of the Cross and down the path leading to the Blessed Virgin's Grotto. Beyond the shrine the path continued past the cemetery, the chicken coops and opened up into a hay field that sloped toward the Hudson River. In the colder weather he wore an Irish cap and pulled the brim tightly down over his eyes. He repeated his hikes to the river during the evening manual labor.

Although one of the virtues I was supposed to practice was "modesty of the eyes" and not watch what others were doing, his absence was noticeable. Novices, who were ordinarily quiet during manual labor, would converse softly; they knew Brother Gabriel wasn't around to supervise and reprimand. One of the few possessions the brothers had allowed me to keep was my 35mm camera, and one evening I hid the camera inside my robe and followed him, If he saw me while he was smoking I would pretend I didn't see him. He would ignore me and I would ignore him. If he said something he would have to reveal what he was doing. I walked slowly along the path until I spotted him lying under a tree, his head propped under his right hand, his back toward me as he looked out at the Hudson River. I hurriedly snapped one picture and returned to the Novitiate. Since I knew the junior novice who had taken my place as the newspaper photographer I snuck the roll of film to him and he developed it. I never showed the photo to anyone, but in it Brother Gabriel looks quite peaceful, gazing at the Hudson River with a cigarette in his right hand. Perhaps what I needed to advance in the practice of meditation was a good cigarette.

Every morning after manual labor we washed up and reported to the common room where Brother Gabriel lectured us about a religious topic. Often he'd remark that advancing in the spiritual life meant conquering our weaknesses and our shortcomings. The phrase often used, both in the Juniorate and in the novitiate, was "striving for perfection," an impossible goal, but Brother Gabriel's attitude focused on the act of striving rather than the goal of perfection. I knew he meant what he said, he endured his own faults, and for his honesty alone I liked him. While his demeanor always kept him aloof from the novices, when I spoke with him in reddition he expressed true interest in my spiritual growth. He advised me to stay grounded and avoid being a slave to pious practices and the shackles of scrupulosity. He stressed the essence of a good spiritual life combines prayer with self-examination, reading sound theological authors and reflecting on what I read.

The faculty of the novitiate also included Brother Albinus of Mary who many of us knew from our freshman year of high school in the Day Juniorate. His interests tended toward history and he lectured us on the evolution of the Catholic

Church and the role the Church Fathers had in its development. We read *The City of God* by Saint Augustine (the first memoir), the writings of St. John Baptist de La Salle, our founder, and commentaries on the *Summa Theologica* of St. Thomas Aquinas. A multi-volume English translation of the Latin *Summa* was available in the spiritual reading library. I learned one style of argument from reading Aquinas. For each theological proposition Aquinas started his discussion with the opposite proposition, the objections, and argued their possible truth by citing scripture, previous church writings and Aristotle. At the end of the discussion Aquinas always concluded by writing, "But I say that..." and then Aquinas would state the correct position of the Catholic Church and indicate the errors of his previous arguments. The two things I learned from reading Aquinas was the importance of understanding someone else's point of view and a theological position wasn't necessarily correct just because a person argued it well.

Brother Albinus openly criticized how many of our schools had lost their focus. He believed in a rigorous religious curriculum combined with a study of history and politics. In 1960 a decision had been made that the brothers would concentrate their efforts in secondary schools rather than grammar schools. The district government denied requests to staff additional grammar schools in the archdiocese of New York. Instead the brothers assumed the administration of more secondary schools: St. Joseph's High School in West New York, New Jersey, and Queen of Peace High School in North Arlington, New

Jersey. They closed De La Salle Institute on 74ᵗʰ Street and replaced it with a new high school, Christian Brothers Academy in Lincroft, New Jersey. Each of these schools sponsored major sports programs. Brother Albinus didn't agree with this development and remarked that the Brothers concentrated on running gymnasiums with schools attached.

Brother Albinus's office was centrally located at the foot of the stairs leading up to the dormitories. He maintained an open door policy and gladly entertained any novice who just wanted to chat. Every day, as soon as the mail arrived, Brother Albinus would sit at his desk poring over the *New York Times*. He would drop the sports pages into the garbage can that he always referred to as his "circular file."

In the spring of 1960 Brother Albinus followed the presidential primaries. For weeks before the primary, when we walked around the property after dinner in the evening, Brother Albinus talked incessantly about the imminent West Virginia primary. I learned that when Al Smith, the first Catholic nominated for the presidency, ran on the Democratic ticket in 1928 he couldn't shake his religious beliefs and those values sank his effort to win the Presidency. Brother Albinus noted that John Kennedy had brilliantly defused the identical issue in West Virginia by comparing tolerance versus intolerance, but when necessary Kennedy injected his Catholic beliefs directly into the debate. In a speech in West Virginia on April 13, 1960 Kennedy remarked, "Is anyone going to tell me I lost this primary battle forty-two years ago when I was baptized?"[7]

While Brother Albinus recognized that American politics might radically change, I, like most novices, showed little interest. On the morning of May 11, 1960, I walked by Brother Albinus's office. He was holding the *New York Times* and waved to me to come into the office. He said, "Did you hear what happened yesterday?" I said no, thinking I had missed some scandal in the novitiate or that some novice had fluked. He pointed to the front page of the *New York Times*. John Kennedy had won the West Virginia democratic primary. I can't remember him being more excited. For a week he exuded happiness as if he had created the primary strategy himself and had managed the get-out-the-vote operation directly from his tiny office in the Novitiate.

He realized he was experiencing a historical event, Kennedy defeating the more popular Senator Humphrey from Minnesota in a primary, and with that victory opening the distinct possibility that a Roman Catholic might be elected president of the United States. I never imagined that less than four years later another event involving John Kennedy would change everyone's world forever.

The faculty of the novitiate included Brother Gabriel and Brother Albinus, but a third person, Brother Benilde James, affected our lives deeply. He had taught me English in the Juniorate but his other responsibility included training the novices to lead the liturgical singing at mass and other ceremonies. While he liked literature, he loved music more, especially Gregorian Chant, the official music of the Roman Catholic liturgy. When he had led us at music practice in the Juniorate, we sang the common prayers of the Mass: the Gloria, a hymn of praise, the Credo, a hymn of belief, and the Agnus Dei, a petition for God's forgiveness. In the Novitiate, however, the novices practiced the more intricate pieces: the Introit, the introductory prayer, the Collects, prayers in response to scriptural readings, and all the antiphons that would be sung at Vespers, the first night prayer before dinner, and Compline, the last prayer just before retiring for the night. Cantors stood and intoned the first verse for many of these prayers and Brother Benilde selected me as one of the cantors. During some spiritual reading sessions, I would retire to the large chapel with three other brothers. Brother Benilde joined us as we practiced singing the selections for Sunday's high mass.

Gregorian Chant is sung *a cappella* and the introits of the major feasts, even though they are sung without musical accompaniment, are melodious and memorable. The Christmas liturgy, the feast of the Nativity of Our Lord, lasted most of Christmas morning. We sang not one but three masses: one at midnight, one at dawn, and the mass of the day at nine o' clock in the morning. I can still sing from memory the opening notes from the introit of the mass of the day, the *Puer Natus Est*, A Child is Born to Us. While we practiced often, we only sang the actual masses once. However, we sang one mass so often we didn't need to practice it—the Requiem.

When a brother died we celebrated the burial mass immediately the next morning. On November 21, 1959, we celebrated the feast of the Presentation of the Blessed Virgin with a high mass at 6:30. This event concerning the Blessed Virgin is not found in the canonical scriptures but appears in some of the apocryphal writings. The feast celebrates the presentation of Mary to the temple priests when she was three years old. It was the official feast of the Juniorate and would have been a holiday even for novices, but at ten that morning we all gathered again in the chapel and sang a Requiem Mass for one of the ancient brothers who died the previous day. That afternoon another ancient brother died and the following morning we did it all over again, celebrating a regular mass early and another Requiem Mass at ten.

The music of the Requiem Mass is somber and funereal. There are few high octave notes in the introit, *Requiem Aeternam*. Many of the lower notes are held for a long time and the melody resembles wailing. At the end of the mass one of the most famous Gregorian hymns is sung, the *Dies Irae*, a solemn rhyming poem from the 13th century. At the conclusion of the service, as the catafalque is wheeled down the aisle and out to the cemetery, the short antiphon *In Paradisum* is sung repeatedly as the entire congregation makes its way to the cemetery for the burial service. Its jaunty melody sounds almost festive and transforms the liturgical atmosphere from mourning the dead to the jubilation of a person entering into heaven. At the age of nineteen I participated in burying a lot of people.

The most impressive liturgy at Barrytown, however, was the Easter Vigil service. Everyone—novices, junior novices, even the ancients who were infirm—gathered in a circle outside the large chapel a half hour before midnight on Holy Saturday. The celebrant, usually Father Dobranski, started a fire from flint stone since the blaze represented a new beginning, a resurrection. The priest inscribed the Paschal candle with the Greek letters, alpha and omega, Christ as Beginning and End, and the four digits of the *Anno Domini*, the year of our Lord. After the Pascal candle blessing, the priest picked a burning branch from the fire and lit the candle. Carrying our own unlit candles, we processed into the dark vestibule of the large chapel. The Paschal candle provided the only light. Surrounded by darkness and wearing our black robes, we could hardly see in front of us and the light from the candle reflected off the priest's white vestments. As the front doors to the large chapel opened, the celebrant intoned, "Lumen Christi." The congregation responded, "Deo Gratias." The custom demanded we sing as loudly as possible, and our voices reverberated off the vestibule walls. We processed into the nave, and as we walked, our candles were lit from the flame of the Paschal candle. In the middle of the chapel the celebrant stopped, raised the Paschal candle and intoned "Lumen Christi" a second time but in a higher key. Again we responded "Deo Gratias" and gradually the chapel brightened as we passed the flame from one candle to another. Finally, the celebrant reached the sanctuary and recited "Lumen Christi" a third time in yet a higher key.

When we answered "Deo Gratias," all the lights in the chapel were turned on. In the Roman Catholic liturgy this was a most impressive ceremony; it was filled with simple yet emotional symbolism—darkness into light. Easter in the Christian churches is the highest ranking feast. It is the theological crux of Christianity; we believe that Christ was raised from the dead. As St. Paul has written in his first letter to the Corinthians, "If Christ is not risen, our faith is in vain" (1 Corinthians 14:17).

One thing I miss from that time is the Gregorian Chant. In today's liturgy these prayers have been translated into English but when they are sung, the English words don't fit the Latin notes. Now, at the Paschal Vigil, the celebrant sings "The Light of Christ" as the procession enters the church. The Latin phrase contains only two words, "Lumen Christi" and neither needs translation. The word "lumen" is on most packaging of incandescent bulbs and can only be understood as meaning light. The English translation contains two unnecessary words, "the" and "of," and the additional words dilute the melody. Today when I attend the Easter Vigil liturgy I quietly intone "Lumen Christi" and while everyone else responds with "Thanks be to God" I am singing *Deo Gratias* softly. As I enter the church, I am sad the lights are already on.

Chapter 12

In 1960, my novitiate year, the Christian Brothers of the New York District underwent drastic organizational changes in the schools they administered. The superiors of the district chose to shift the brothers' educational mission from grammar schools to high schools and attempted to simplify the complexity of the organization.

The Christian Brothers had seven districts in the United States. The New York District, the largest, with more than seven hundred brothers in forty-four schools in seven states, stretched from Providence, Rhode Island, to Detroit, Michigan. In 1958, the provincial council of the district, under the leadership of Brother Anthony John, who had assumed the position of Brother Visitor in 1955, decided to split the district into two parts. The dividing line ran straight through New York City. Schools in Brooklyn, Queens and Long Island joined schools in Connecticut, Rhode Island, Massachusetts and New Hampshire to form a new district with the name Long Island – New England district, the LINE district. Schools in the

Bronx and Manhattan, upstate New York, New Jersey and Michigan remained in the New York District.

The LINE district bought a mansion on Ocean Road in Narragansett, Rhode Island, and they built a novitiate on the property for the brothers in that district. Delays in construction forced the first group of novices, scheduled to arrive in the summer of 1959, to go to Barrytown. The new novitiate was completed in the late fall of 1959 but the brothers decided to delay the move to Narragansett until after Christmas. On Thursday January 7, 1960 a bus arrived at the novitiate in Barrytown to take those novices whose school of origin was in the newly formed district and transport them to Narragansett.

It was the day after the feast of the Epiphany, officially known as the presentation of Christ to the Gentiles although major image of the feast is the three Magi arriving at Bethlehem. Someone selected January 7 on purpose for its symbolism; the day marked the end of the Christmas season and the resumption of ordinary time in the liturgy—a new beginning. It is the time when the Christian liturgy contains no major feasts like Easter, Pentecost or Christmas. Father Dobranski celebrated a solemn high mass—and added special collects reserved for those Christians about to undertake a journey. Expectations ran high that morning; the departing novices felt uncertain about their journey; those remaining wondered about those leaving and the absence it would create in the novitiate. I envied the novices leaving; the trip sounded like an adventure. After an introductory reading at breakfast, Brother Gabriel rang a little cowbell that sat on his table and intoned "Benedicamus Domino," blessed is the Lord. We were surprised. We responded "Deo Gratias," thanks be to God, and then, after a few words from Brother Gabriel about this being a last breakfast of all the novices, he allowed us to talk for the remainder of the meal. When conversation at a meal was allowed we called it a "beni," a shortening of the word "benidicamus," but a "beni" at breakfast was unheard of even on a unique day like that.

After breakfast the novices who were traveling to Narragansett skipped manual labor. They went to the dormitory and carried their bags out to the waiting bus in the circle in front of the large chapel. Since I would remain at Barrytown my assignment included clearing the breakfast tables and cleaning the dishes. When we set the tables for lunch we set only half the number of places and moved the extra tables to a far corner of the refectory.

The bus driver loaded the luggage into the storage compartments. Around ten o'clock we gathered around the statue of St. Michael the archangel in the center of the circle and recited a prayer for the safety of those traveling. Then they boarded the bus, and I watched it leave the novitiate, turn left onto Barrytown Road and head east to Rhode Island. When I returned inside, I felt the emptiness of the building. Some of my best friends were on that bus and I wondered if I would ever see them again. Brother Gabriel attempted to dispel this mood. He must have felt it himself and he tinkered with our routine by reassigning sleeping cells in the dormitory so that all the remaining novices slept in the lower dorm on the third floor. The upper dorm remained vacant. One of the unexpected advantages of twenty-five fewer novices occurred the next morning—the wait to take a shower was shorter.

Brother Gabriel also reassigned us to different desks in the common room and told us to take an empty desk and move it next to our own. The width of the aisles doubled and the spaciousness of the new arrangement made it feel gloomier. Brother Benilde came over that evening from the Juniorate to assist us with some new selections of Gregorian Chant. We were saddened by the departure of the others and he allowed us to talk about how we felt instead of practicing singing.

By the end of January the charm of being in the novitiate began to wear off. Each day was identical to the next: rise before the sun, recite morning prayers, celebrate the Eucharist, read, work and pray. High Mass on Sunday provided some diversion but as the weather turned colder and stayed cold, I went outside less and developed the cloistered form of cabin fever; why was I here? Maybe I should be someplace else, although I wasn't sure of where it I might want to be. I had lived in Barrytown for more almost four years, the prime of my teen-years and wondered what I had given up.

Twenty-two of us remained at Barrytown after the other novices left. Soon the number was under twenty. Tom Nearney and Tom Condon, both of whom had been in the day juniorate with me, left the novitiate in the winter of 1960. Including me, only seven remained from those who had attended the day juniorate four years before.

That winter I questioned my vocation for the first time. The life of a religious had lost its glamour. The predictable routine allowed me to ask many questions but I found few answers and I made an appointment with Brother Gabriel to tell him how I felt. I went into his office and said, "I think I've lost my vocation." He didn't reply. I rephrased my feeling. "I think I might want to leave the novitiate." Still he said nothing.

Brother Gabriel never pretended he would decide whether or not a novice had a vocation. What I wanted from him, however, was his view of who I was and whether I should be here. Did he think I had a vocation? After all, he was the director of novices; he should know. Wasn't that his job? Many are called but few are chosen, and he chaired the selection committee. Without his approval I wouldn't be allowed to take temporary vows at the end of the novitiate year.

Like Brother Eugene, when I spoke with him in the Brother's House at St. John's, Brother Gabriel's only advice was to pray for guidance. God would let me know if He had chosen me. I was disappointed with his answer and I didn't pursue it with him again. He never questioned me about why I remained, but I did.

Brother Gabriel continued his lectures about the religious vows. The second one was the vow of chastity. This name is a slight misnomer. All Christians are called to be chaste, as we were reminded constantly, but when the lectures concerned chastity the emphasis was on our sexuality, we would practice celibacy. In the female religious order a nun became a "bride of Christ." No such metaphor existed for males. Every brother director in the juniorate who lectured to us about this topic danced around it. The common expression used was the reference in St. Paul's letter to the Corinthians that our bodies were temples of the Holy Spirit. They quoted this verse often. If we had any doubt what it meant, the next verse made it clear. "The immoral man sins against his own body." (1 Corinthians 6:19). Sometimes they warned us directly that we should not engage in self-abuse. The word onanism arose occasionally, after the character Onan in the Book of Genesis, but I don't ever remember the word "masturbation" being used. To me the vow of chastity always seemed wrapped up in sexuality, I would forgo marriage and therefore abstain from a sexual relationship, but the intention of the vow was nobler; a religious would remain celibate in order to be able to serve God more fully. I would take the vow of celibacy and forego marriage. I would dedicate both my mind and body to serving God. The Catholic Church built the logic to this argument by arguing that Christ never married and implied that marriage, while it was one of the seven sacraments, ranked lower than celibacy.

What was really going on in my mind was the impossibility of suppressing one's sexual appetite. It might have been easier to curb my desire for food. In order to help ease the suppression, I was urged to practice "mortification of the flesh." Standing up voluntarily to eat dinner, not putting salt on food, kneeling on the stone floor of the chapel instead of in the pew were only a few of the suggestions to toughen my resolve.

Nevertheless, the brothers often quoted Christ's admonition to his disciples in the Garden of Gethsemane that "the spirit is willing but the flesh is weak." This was the reason for the strict prohibition of developing a "particular friendship." There were hardly any females at Barrytown. Girls appeared only when families visited and someone's sister walked around the grounds. Most of us who entered the novitiate were heterosexual, as I was, but I would learn later that a minority were homosexual. It didn't matter. Both orientations were treated as afflictions—heterosexuality challenged celibacy and homosexuality was intrinsically evil. Sexual desires, of all persuasions, had to be curbed. What would have been natural for me I now had to treat as undesirable because I chose to be celibate. What was unnatural, homosexuality, at least that was the official doctrine of the Catholic Church, had to be curbed also. I had to suppress my heterosexuality and others had to suppress their homosexuality. It made little difference what the orientation was. It was probably more difficult for them.

The official dogma of the Catholic Church is that homosexuality is immoral, but the reason most Brothers withdrew from the order was because the vow of celibacy was too demanding. Whether a person was heterosexual or homosexual didn't really make any difference. Either way, the need for a close intimate relationship with another person was stronger than the desire to live one's life without such a relationship.

A few years later, in 1968, the Christian Brothers commissioned a study of the order. The results were published in a book entitled *The Committed* by William Ammentorp of the University of Minnesota.[8] On page 169 Ammentorp states that "the free and easy mannerisms of the religious frequently mask a basic unwillingness to form deep and significant personal relationships." For me this was partially true. I was unwilling to foster relationships because I was discouraged from forming them.

Harvey Cox is supposed to have said; "Not to decide is to decide." What he really said was "Somewhere deep down we know that in the final analysis we do decide things and that even our decisions to let someone else decide are really our decisions."[9] Brother Gabriel didn't let me fall into that trap. He knew his role as director well. His was to lead and explain. My role was to follow and accept but whatever I did I would decide for myself. I decided to stay although maybe I decided not to leave. I think the latter was truer.

Chapter 13

For a boy brought up in the northwest
Bronx, a spring after a snowy winter arrived
differently in Barrytown.

In December 1947 when I was six years
old, the northeast United States endured a huge
snowstorm that shut down New York City for two
days after Christmas. The snowfall measured
twenty-six inches and I was quite happy to use the
new sled I received from Santa Claus. Summit
Place, a hilly cross street between Heath Avenue
and Kingsbridge Terrace, never even got plowed
and I sledded down the hill and straight into Heath
Avenue. Mr. Johnson, aware of the danger of us
being hit by a bus going up Heath Avenue, spread
the burnt ashes from the coal furnace across the
bottom of Summit Place. The ashes acted like
glue and stopped my sled at the bottom of the hill.
Cars disappeared, buried under snow, sidewalks
remained unshoveled and people walked in the
middle of the street. In the warm spring, New

York City snow melted, ran down the curbs and flowed into the sewer like little waterfalls.

In Barrytown, however, melting snow had nowhere to go but into the ground which could only absorb so much before becoming totally saturated. As the temperature increased, so did the amount of mud. During the early spring when I was in the Juniorate, the brothers forbade us to walk on the football or baseball fields until they completely dried out. Some manual labor assignments involved maintaining the dirt roadways leading to the barns. We filled the potholes with gravel and smoothed the road. When walking around the property, I needed a good pair of boots. After I came in from outside, I had take off my boots and clap the soles to remove the mud so it wouldn't be tracked into the dormitory. One of the most undesirable manual labor assignments in spring was sweeping and mopping the corridors that led out to the ball fields; mud was everywhere.

While sports had dominated my recreation time in the Juniorate, Brother Conrad Leo, the Latin teacher, had encouraged another activity— bird watching. Not many boys took to the idea of accompanying him as he sloshed his way across the cow pastures and down the hill toward the pond. He pointed out the brown headed cowbird and told us to think about how the bird got its name. "Look at the stupid birds. They peck around the ground right underneath the cow's tail," he said. Brother Leo, always the teacher, initiated us into ornithology by having us identify the obviously named birds: the red-wing blackbird (dozens of them swooped around the marshes near the pond), the bluebird and the pileated woodpecker, a crow size bird with a spectacular red crest. I would hear it drumming into a dead tree a hundred yards away before spotting it. Hundreds of chimney swifts, tailless birds that resembled cigars with wings, dipped and dove in the corn fields as they feasted on thousands of insects. He taught us how to use binoculars. I easily spotted birds that perched on tree limbs and fences but some species—wrens, sparrows and thrushes—constantly fidgeted under shrubs and proved difficult to identify. I soon learned how to follow a bird's flight using only the binoculars and I could finger the focal dials and change the clarity of the field depth without having to look at the settings.

I became an avid bird watcher, and by the time I went to the Novitiate I was allowed to keep a pair of binoculars for myself and make notations of sightings in my own copy of Robert Tory Petersen's *A Field Guide to the Birds,* the Bible for bird watchers. In the spring of 1960, with only twenty novices, playing organized baseball was impossible—a few disliked sports—so I spent much of my free time hiking around the property searching for birds. I had survived the dreary winter and while I was still in limbo about my vocation, I had remained. The long walks allowed me the solitude to reflect and think. Despite all the distractions of nature around me, I seemed more able to mediate while watching birds than I did kneeling in chapel. A verse in the Gospel of St. Matthew stuck in my mind: "Do not be anxious for your life"; the verse is followed by "Look at the birds of the air. They do not sow or reap or gather into barns but your Heavenly Father feeds them." I watched birds and concluded that by remaining a brother I'd be taken care of.

With a pair of binoculars around my neck and Petersen's book stuck in my rear pocket, I wandered everywhere on the property. I hiked past the barns into the woods and as far north as Cruger Island Road that led west to that island in the Hudson River and east onto the campus of Bard College. When I tired of watching ducks, herons and cormorants, I turned my attention to the cars and trucks on the recently completed bridge that connected the city of Kingston in Ulster county to the town of Rhinecliff in Dutchess County.

One Saturday morning the previous spring, all the seniors in the Juniorate had boarded a bus and crossed that bridge to take the Scholastic Aptitude Test at Kingston High School. We hadn't taken any practice exams and the only preparation for the test was making sure we had several freshly sharpened No. 2 pencils. We got off the bus in front of the high school and walked as a group into the classrooms. The Kingston High School students, also taking the test, stared at us, not knowing quite what to make of two dozen high school boys wearing black shoes, slacks and dress shirts on a Saturday morning. I remember looking at them in the same way; teenage fashion had changed in the three years I was in the Juniorate; lots of clashing colors on the girls' skirts and much longer hair on the boys.

On the verbal section of the exam I thought I did fairly well with the vocabulary. Each day for three years Brother Benilde had

152

taught us the meaning and etymology of a word from the vocabulary section of the Readers Digest. I fared less well with the analogies.

In the mathematics section I felt more confident but I never found out any results of the exam until the next spring in the Novitiate. I don't remember being given a reason for taking the test. Our last two college years would be at The Catholic University of America in Washington D.C. and perhaps their admission policies required taking the test, or even doing well on it, but it was never an issue. Our first two years in college had already been planned. The freshman year would be in Troy, New York, and our second year at De La Salle College in Avondale, Maryland, on the border of the northeast section of Washington, D.C.

Brother Bernard, one of the French teachers in the Juniorate, had been transferred to the Scholasticate, as De La Salle College was known, to study for his Ph.D in French Literature. He returned to the Novitiate at Barrytown and met with each novice privately to discuss what our courses would be in the first year of college. He started with a review of my high school transcript and told me I had scored well on the SAT although I never learned the actual scores.

Certainly the Brothers discussed each of us among themselves and what they thought we could accomplish academically. In the Scholasticate, we would be preparing to be teachers. I scored just over 500 on the verbal part of the SAT test and in the low 600s on the math section. My average verbal score on the SAT combined with my mediocre grades in Latin and

French in the Juniorate meant I didn't have a future as a language or classical studies major. My final grade in French had been 75 and I hadn't taken a Latin course since my sophomore year. At the end of the year in the Juniorate the school newspaper published a supplement with the biographies of the graduates. Each graduate signed a copy for the undergraduates. Hugh Canning wrote to me; "If you think you had a hard time in French think of me." Hugh dreaded what I found easy; while many abhorred geometry, I struggled with French.

The Brothers already had too many history and English majors. So, since I had scored well on the SAT math and my final trigonometry grade was 90, Brother Bernard told me my major would be theoretical physics. Brother Bernard and others planned what I would study in college depending on the teaching needs of the high schools. Since the brothers' new focus concerned running high schools, the demand for science teachers soared and I would help fulfill that need.

Brother Bernard outlined my college course for my freshman year at Hillside Hall in Troy, New York. The Brothers expected a lot and it would not be an easy curriculum—I would take six courses totaling twenty credits in the fall term: English Composition, Intermediate French, General Organic Chemistry, College Algebra, Western European History and Religious Education.

I never questioned this decision about what college courses I would take or what my major would be. The vow of obedience would determine my behavior and whatever the brothers suggested I study I would embrace. If I did question it, I would be told "This is what you will study" and I must accept it as part of my vow of obedience. I never found this vow difficult, even though as a child my mother claimed my main fault was disobedience. For almost five years, I had obeyed my religious superiors faithfully. I slept where I was told, took my assigned place at the dinner table, sat at the desk in the common room, performed whatever manual labor was assigned, and prayed in a certain pew. When bells rang I got up. When they rang again I went to chapel to pray. At night I went to bed at the sound of a bell. It didn't seem strange to me that the Brothers would choose my course of study.

Brother Gabriel encouraged me to make my own decision about whether or not I should remain in the Novitiate but I did not choose my course of studies. The brothers decided my major and that decision would determine my future: who my classmates would be, who I would study with and who would become my friends. The monastic routine made the daily decisions of life; I chose the lifestyle.

St. La Salle modeled the Christian Brothers on the monastic tradition of the three traditional vows—poverty, chastity and obedience—and these two minor ones. The minor vows I would take at the end of the Novitiate included the vow of stability and the vow of teaching the poor gratuitously.

In the 17th century religious orders needed a vow of stability to prevent a religious from wandering from one monastic community to another. One problem as far back as the 12th century involved monks who didn't like one monastery or clashed with an abbot's personality. The religious would leave abruptly to join another community or would switch orders from the Dominicans to the Franciscans. The problem, common enough in monastic history, led to the creation of this vow so that monks in a particular monastery would remain there. For the brothers, it meant accepting whatever assignment you were given, whatever school you were sent to. I couldn't choose where I would teach; I would teach where I was needed.

The brothers observed the vow of teaching the poor gratuitously mostly in the breach. Only those brothers who accepted assignments in the missions, that is, in the schools in Addis Ababa, Ethiopia, and Nairobi, Kenya, taught without remuneration from the students. American students paid tuition.

With my immediate future solidified, the remainder of my time in the Novitiate involved waiting. Spring turned to summer and in late June a new group of postulants arrived from the Juniorate and from the high schools where the Brothers taught. The influx of more people gave the Novitiate a new spirit and the summer passed quickly. The postulants received their robes on September 7, 1960, and the next day I pronounced my first vows. These vows would last for one year. After one year I would renew the vows for two years and then for three years. After six years of temporary vows I would profess final vows to last for my entire life.

On September 9, 1960, a bus arrived at the Novitiate to take us to Hillside Hall in Troy, New

York. We were joined there by the two dozen novices from Narragansett who had left Barrytown eight months earlier. My academic work would soon start and would prove even more difficult than I anticipated.

Chapter 14

What I remember most about Hillside Hall are the dozens of tiny sinks.

The Brothers had administered an orphanage in Troy, New York since 1850 and the cornerstone of the Troy Catholic Male Orphan Asylum was blessed on June 24, 1866. In 1927 the name was changed to Hillside School.[10] It was an apt choice for the five story structure perched on the eastern hills of Troy. From the common room window on the fourth floor I could see the city of Albany, the capital of New York, to the southwest, and the Hudson River, shrinking to a narrow creek as it wandered north into the Adirondack Mountains. The dormitory on the top floor ran the entire length of the building and in the corridor outside the dormitory, attached to both walls, were porcelain sinks designed for boys no taller than three feet. When I rinsed shaving cream off my face, I had to bend deeply at my waist as if I was trying to touch my toes; I could barely reach into the tiny basin, only twenty inches off the floor and holding less than two quarts of water. The dried-out rubber stopper attached to a rusted chain had long ago lost its ability to keep the water in the sink, so I kept the tap running to rinse the razor.

The brother director, Brother Berthulian Joseph, ran the community as I had expected. His reputation had preceded him; I anticipated an austere personality, a mouth that rarely smiled, detective eyes always searching for a crime; he didn't disappoint me. He presided as if he was running an extension of the Novitiate year and he found fault with everyone. Fortunately, my stay at Hillside lasted only nine months, from September 1960 until June 1961, and I spent the majority of my day engrossed in studying.

I avoided Brother Joseph as much as I could and tried to lose myself in the heavy schedule of the fall semester. My academic load consisted of six courses totaling twenty credits. With meager recreational facilities—a handball court at the rear of the building and a pool table in the basement recreation room—I could do little else but study. Brother Joseph placed severe restrictions on leaving the property, so I couldn't wander around looking for birds. My binoculars collected dust on the small bureau in the dormitory.

After four years in the Juniorate and one year in the Novitiate, I anticipated being taught by excellent teachers and I was rewarded with brilliant examples of instruction. Another brother on the faculty with the same name Joseph, Brother Cassian Joseph, spent much of his day studying for a Ph.D in chemical engineering at Rensselaer Polytechnic Institute in Troy, about two miles

159

north of Hillside Hall. When he graduated from RPI in 1964, he was assigned to teach chemistry at Manhattan College in the Bronx, where he remained for four decades until he died in 2007 on May 1, the memorial feast of his namesake, St. Joseph the Worker.

When he wasn't studying at RPI, Brother Joseph taught us general inorganic chemistry. The sign of a great teacher is that he makes it look so easy and I had little difficulty. I could recite the valences of elements as rapidly as I could recite New York Yankee statistics and balancing chemical equations was as easy as calculating Brother Peter's mental arithmetic questions in the seventh grade at St. John's. Understanding the periodic table was never a problem; I got an A in both the fall and the spring sections. Brother Joseph lulled me into believing I possessed the qualities of a scholar.

Many years later Brother Joseph, like many of us, would withdraw from the Brothers but the administration at Manhattan College acted wisely when they kept him on the faculty. He became a legend teaching at Manhattan where, although it is trivial to say it, his students admired him.

In the spring of 2007, when he was confined to bed and dying, former students from Manhattan College visited Professor Joseph Reynolds (his secular name) at his house in the nearby Woodlawn section of the Bronx, just east from Manhattan College. They sat on his bed and talked to him, helped him eat and told him their stories. At his wake I noticed that there was no physical body present and, knowing that he was a tireless teacher, I thought he might have asked to be laid out in the chemistry lab. He had repeatedly announced that he would never retire. Like many of us, he found his true vocation was at the front of a classroom.

The Mass the next day in the chapel at Manhattan College, again without a body present, was a memorial rather than a Requiem. The liturgy felt like a celebration of life, which is exactly the title of the ceremony on the front cover of the leaflet distributed at the service. Dylan Thomas's poem *And Death Shall Have No Dominion* was printed on the back cover and reiterated the first scriptural reading from St. Paul's epistle to the Romans. "Death shall no longer have dominion over him" (Romans 6:9). His family could only wish that death had no dominion but it does. The more comforting line to me in Dylan Thomas's poem read "Though lovers be lost love shall not."

If the dead could tell us something, high on the list would be the recognition and honor for their work. Joseph Reynolds, wherever his body was, was not disappointed. The congregation was filled with former students like me. While I was also a member of the Christian Brothers, I did not attend this service because he was a colleague but because he was my teacher at Hillside Hall those many years ago. The impression he made on me never faded. At the end of the mass as the family processed out of the chapel, his present Manhattan College students, dozens of them, lined the center aisle from the altar railing to the front door as an honor guard. There could not have been a more fitting display of affection for a great teacher.

One of Joseph Reynolds's favorite quotations about teaching, and also a favorite of mine, is from Act I of Robert Bolt's play, *A Man for All Seasons*, when Thomas More gives unsolicited advice to Richard Rich who yearned for a career in the English court.[11]

"Why not be a teacher?" More asks. "You'd be a fine teacher. Perhaps a great one."

"And if I was, who would know it?" Rich replies.

"You, your pupils, your friends, God; not a bad public," More responds.

It was evident that Joseph Reynolds's students knew how great a teacher he was. Long before any of them were ever born I had already known. I stayed in my pew but had an urge to step into the aisle and join the students.

ᗛᗕ

At Hillside Hall, however, while I breezed through my chemistry assignments, my problems with the French language continued to mount. Brother Cecilian of Mary, an energetic but often an absentminded man, taught Intermediate French. He was fluent in several languages and often overlooked teaching the class, instead rhapsodizing on the lyrics of some minor French poet. He insisted we always ask a question in the language being taught. One morning he started the lecture speaking German. We tried to stop him using English and French but not until someone could recall the German word for "stop" did Brother Cecilian realize his error.

At the start of some classes he'd review the translation he had finished the day before. For me it wasn't very helpful the second time around and for the first time in my life I failed a course. The expression "I have no idea what you are talking about" was quite apropos. Even though I received an "F" in the fall section of French Literature, that failure didn't affect my schedule in the spring semester. I continued taking Intermediate French, knowing I would have to make up the failed semester in the summer, and inexplicably achieved a grade of B in the spring section, but my worry about passing French distracted me from another course I should have paid more attention to—that spring I failed Calculus I. Only a year into college and I had already failed two courses.

A second teacher at Hillside Hall, Brother Eulogius Austin who taught A Survey of Western European History, can only be described as unconventional and unpredictable—a brilliant eccentric with the rare ability to construct jokes about guillotines. On the first day, he walked into class and announced that the curriculum would span history from Adam to Eisenhower. By the end of the first week we were being regaled about the Babylonian court of Nebuchodonosor but his lectures wandered, pursuing digressions from digressions and, by the end of the year, we had hardly made it past the Protestant Reformation. If Brother Eulogius Austin—he was always referred to by both his religious names—had ever needed a paying job he would have thrived as a stand-up

163

comic. I was sure the director, the other Brother Joseph, ever the killjoy, cringed when he heard our European History class constantly erupting in laughter. Brother Eulogius Austin deadpanned remarks about how the Mohawk Indians—as he pointed dramatically out the western window to the Mohawk Valley—were superior hunter-gatherers over the Iroquois precisely because they carved out aluminum canoes and titanium arrows. When he spoke about any historical figure—Charlemagne, Attila the Hun, Martin Luther—he recited obscure facts so nonchalantly that I thought he might have had dinner with them the night before. His droll sense of humor combined with an encyclopedic knowledge meant that each class would be a performance. If his self-deprecation wasn't enough, Brother Eulogius Austin had one characteristic that added to the unpredictability of his lectures—he stuttered. He was conscious of it—but never self-conscious—and he warned us to be patient and bear with him whenever he became tongue-tied during class. The first couple of times I experienced his stuttering I felt bad. His mouth froze and the only noise he made sounded prehistorically guttural. It occurred frequently—every fifteen or twenty minutes in a lecture—but he never acted embarrassed so I soon ignored it. He wanted to overcome his inability to get a word out; he said he would never use a substitute word and he would always keep trying to finish what he was saying; often he did. But, on one occasion, as he lectured about the Battle of Waterloo and the inferiority complex of Napoleon he froze. At the end of one sentence he had two words left when he started to stutter. From the context of the

lecture we all knew what the two words were—
Napoleon Bonaparte—but he got stuck on the first
syllable of the first name and kept repeating "Na-
Na-Na-Na." He couldn't get Napoleon's name out
and he must have tried for ten or fifteen seconds.
Finally, exasperated, he gave up trying to
pronounce the name and said, "That little fuckin'
Frenchman." We laughed so hard I thought
Hillside Hall would collapse.

Brother Eulogius Austin watched birds
avidly. He knew I was a birdwatcher and in the
late afternoons he noticed me out on the back
porch with my binoculars searching for birds on
the steep slopes behind Hillside Hall. Even
though I watched birds, Brother Joseph, the
Director, unlike Brother Gabriel in the Novitiate,
didn't grant me the freedom to wander off the
property. On many afternoons I paced the back
porch and saw nothing more than house sparrows
and English starlings in the brush. Brother
Eulogius Austin rewarded my perseverance.

One evening around 5:30, at the time set
apart for Spiritual Reading before dinner, I sat at
my desk in the common room reading. Brother
Eulogius Austin walked in and down the aisle
toward my desk. Instead of his religious habit he
wore casual clothes with his binoculars hung
around his neck. He said nothing but motioned
me to follow him. When we reached the corridor
he whispered, "Go upstairs, change into street
clothes, bring your binoculars and meet me in the
truck outside the kitchen door." I looked at him
strangely; it was highly unorthodox to go to the
dormitory without a good reason and without
getting explicit permission from the Brother

Director. If I was caught by Brother Joseph, I would be severely reprimanded for the violations of that rule, not to mention leaving the property. "Don't worry. I took care of everything. There's buh-buh-buh-buh.." he started but spit it out quickly. "Bufflehead ducks on the Hudson River."

For birdwatchers, buffleheads were heady stuff. They are neither rare nor attractive. As ducks go, their bodies look like they have been crushed in a vise; both their beaks and tails are short. Their beauty is a huge head with a triangle of white from beak to crown. Three of us drove down Monroe Street; Brother Eulogius Austin, another brother who was also a birdwatcher and me. He parked the truck but kept the motor running. We couldn't stay long. Spring evenings in Troy turned colder at sunset and ice floes still packed the river banks. A flock of buffleheads bobbed up and down amid the floating ice. We watched for about ten minutes.

When we returned supper was over. Clean-up had already started but Brother Eulogius Austin had arranged for someone to keep our dinner warm. The three of us sat down without bothering to go put our religious habits back on. Since we were allowed to talk after dinner, the three of us ate, paged through our copies of *Peterson's Guide* to learn more about buffleheads and talked about ducks. Brother Joseph, the Director, never said anything.

While Brother Joseph drilled us in chemical equations and Brother Cecilian rhapsodized about French poets and Brother Eulogius Austin whisked us through the Hundred

Years War in half an hour, Brother Joseph, the Director, lulled us to sleep in Religion class. The course was worth only two college credits but he demanded we spend as much time on his curriculum as any other course. I found it easy: read, write an essay, take a test and try to stay awake. He didn't have the demeanor of our other teachers, his grim personality clashed with the ideas he taught; a Christian shouldn't be that morose.

With my failure of French in the first semester and the impending failure of Calculus I in the second semester, I needed as high a grade as I could earn in Religion to keep my grade point average near three.

When I saw my final grade was a B I found it hard to believe. I had done well on tests so I couldn't figure out why I hadn't received an A. In those days our classes fell under the auspices of the Catholic University of America and their grading system didn't include any in-between grades like B+ or A-.

I knew it would be futile to ask Brother Joseph to reevaluate my scores. He was the kind of person to scan my scores in his grade book and discover he had made an error—the grade I really earned was a C—so I let it be. But I have to admit Brother Joseph did teach me one thing that year for which I have been grateful in my life. I don't need Brother Joseph's chemistry and I ceased learning any more mathematics many years ago but I still think of what Brother Joseph, the Director, taught me.

At the beginning of the school year he assigned us to groups of two or three. Each afternoon, on a rotating basis, he would meet with a group or two for about an hour. He would yell at us, berate us, criticize us, roll his eyes and then demand we do it again. He was trying to teach us to drive using a standard shift.

1960 was the time before seat belts were routinely installed in vehicles and the car we used was a regular four door sedan without instructor controls in the front passenger seat. The driver of the car was in control or, perhaps it would be more accurate to say, was hardly in control.

Very few of us had any experience driving a car, much less using a standard shift, and learning the nuances of controlling the steering wheel with my left hand, shifting gears with my right, lifting my left leg up from the clutch while pressing my right down on the accelerator and doing all this simultaneously seemed impossible to learn. Cars at that time had the gear shift attached to the steering column. Brother Joseph would bark instructions: engage the clutch, pull the gear shift toward your chest then up, disengage the clutch, gear shift down and on it went through third and fourth gear until I finally learned the routine. Only after I had mastered the technique did I get to try it when the car was moving and I couldn't look at my hands. And after that there was reverse gear, parallel parking and three-point turning on a hill.

Only a masochist would attempt to teach fifty nineteen-year-olds how to drive a shift car but Brother Joseph was up to the task. He was firm in his belief that we could do it. Often it was a relief to switch from being the driver to sitting in the back seat and listening to him launch his diatribes at the next student. But Brother Joseph never wavered in his goal. When he thought I was good enough he took me out alone and went through the entire New York State drivers exam. He made me stop on a hill, set the emergency brake on and turn the motor off. Then, I would have to start the motor, release the emergency brake, shift into first gear and drive up the hill. If I rolled back on the hill, even a foot, he made me repeat it until I got it right. I mastered the three-point turns on hills even though the driver's test didn't require it. I don't think any of us failed the driver's exam for New York State that year.

Many times in the classroom when I taught a subject students thought particularly difficult, I used the analogy of learning to drive a stick shift. I told the students that no matter how impossible it felt to learn some idea or skill, they would, in fact, learn it and afterwards they would marvel at how easy it seemed.

At the end of the academic year at Hillside my grades resembled an alphabet soup: four A's, three B's, three C's, and two F's. My grade point average was 2.7, barely a B-. I was an average student among many who achieved straight A's. One evening in the refectory, as I set up the tables for breakfast, Brother Eulogius Austin asked me why I seemed so depressed. I told him I didn't want to be average; I wanted to be better. He said to me "That what's we are. Some of us are just average. Besides," he added, "many brilliant students don't make very good teachers. They can't understand how students struggle to learn."

In the middle of June when there were no more classes, I still had two weeks before I would go to La Salle Military Academy in Oakdale, Long Island for the summer. I brooded for most of those two weeks in the seldom used music room on the second floor of Hillside Hall. I listened to every Beethoven symphony several times a day, but even his "Ode to Joy" in the fourth movement of the Ninth couldn't get me out of my doldrums. Then I discovered another ninth symphony, *From the New World.* It wasn't Beethoven or Mozart and, although at the time I didn't know why Dvořák wrote it, I thought I recognized many of the melodies, especially the song "Goin' Home." Again I pondered whether or not I had a vocation and should myself be going home.

I liked the symphony and listened to it two or three times a day. Its melodies of melancholy and longing never lasted too long, quickly replaced by other melodies that sounded hopeful and buoyant. I decided I still had a vocation and adopted the title as my mantra. In two weeks I would enter my own new world.

Chapter 15

St. La Salle founded the Brothers of the Christian Schools to teach the poor gratuitously as the vow stated. Yet, La Salle Military Academy at Oakdale, Long Island, the summer home of the brothers studying in college, hardly classified as a poor school. Rather, an elite school like LaSalle acted as a financial necessity; while teaching the poor gratuitously was fine in theory, the military academy provided the district with money to do it reality, and the money made at LaSalle supported the less affluent schools in the district. The brothers charged handsomely; some famous graduates included the movie director John Frankenheimer, New Hampshire governor John H. Sununu, and several members of the noted Gambino family, Thomas Gambino and his son.

Closer to home, the children of my first cousin, Barbara Schmidt, the younger daughter of my father's brother Stephen, also attended the school. When I first learned of their attendance I grimaced but realized they represented the Republican side of the family. Barbara's husband,

Robert, served on the Supreme Court of New York State from 1994 to 2008. On the other hand, I knew the children would receive a superior education under the tutelage of the brothers.

I doubted St. La Salle would have approved the word "military" appended to his name. The former name of the school, Clason Military Academy, came from its location at Clason Point in the southeast Bronx but, as enrollment grew after World War I, the facilities became inadequate. [12] The Brothers bought the Oakdale property in 1925 after the death of its owner, a former president of Singer Manufacturing, an aristocrat named Frederick Gilbert "Commodore" Borne. During the 1920s he landscaped the property lavishly. Brother Angelus Gabriel in his book *The Christian Brothers in the United States* describes the grounds in detail. "The lavish beauty of the gardens and groves, rare and exotic shrubs and plants, rolling velvety lawns and picturesque paths, artificial streams and lakes, wide roads shaded by gracefully arching trees of many species, and the majestic entrance of a quarter of a mile roadway flanked by giant evergreens made the estate one of the beauty spots and show places of Long Island."[13]

On a day in late June 1961 I rode a bus through that entrance. I passed the gate house, the gardens to the south next to the tennis courts, the boat house and boat basin, connected to Long Island Sound by a small canal, and around the circle in front of the barracks and school building, St. Joseph's Hall, a four story brick structure, my home for the months of July and August.

My luggage waited for me and I carried it up the grand staircase and through the colonnade to the top floor. I stayed in the cadet's quarters, a large room with beds for six brothers. Besides the bed, we each had a desk where we studied at night since there was no common room, and rather than a bureau, we stored our clothes in a hefty athletic type locker.

I looked out the window overlooking the immense parade ground and the 150 plush acres of land on the edge of Long Island Sound and the panoramic view helped me to forget the claustrophobia of Hillside Hall and my new Director, Brother Bertrand Leo, made it easy to put Brother Berthullian Joseph out of my memory. We always called Brother Leo "Kirby," his secular last name, and even that moniker was abridged to "Kirb." He knew about it, didn't mind it— although we never called him that to his face— because the nickname indicated our affection for him. Brother Leo's homespun personality and his graceful, often self-deprecating laugh endeared him to the scholastics. When annoyed he tried to act stern but his face was made to smile and his grin always returned like elevator doors opening.

Despite the fact that Brother Leo was the Director for over 150 scholastics (the term referred to brothers studying in college) he made a determined effort to know every person individually. In my weekly rendition his questions probed so gently I didn't realize I revealed so much. He rarely criticized me and, even when he did, his kind demeanor never seemed belittling. Most of his spiritual lectures concentrated on the founder's writings and his interest in making St.

La Salle relevant to the brothers of the 20th century inspired him to write a short biography entitled *I, John Baptist De La Salle*. He authored the book in the first person pretending he was St. La Salle reincarnated and I'm sure he felt LaSalle's presence when he wrote. One sentence stood out for me; when Brother Leo described St. La Salle's personality, he really described himself. Brother Leo wrote that "I never really considered myself an intellectual—only a practical man who did what he had to do. I had head knowledge from my studies but I [also] had heart knowledge."[14] Despite the plethora of academic talent of the faculty surrounding him—most members of the faculty studied for their PhDs—Brother Leo understood the necessity of being a counselor.

While Brother Leo's gentle personality eased my relationship with my Brother Director and I felt like he acted more like a spiritual advisor than Brother Joseph—similar to Brother Gabriel's approach in the novitiate—Calculus and French proved upsetting. One of the seniors majoring in mathematics taught me Calculus. He taught well but his difficult tests, combined with the compression of the entire curriculum into six weeks, worried me; what if I failed again? At the end of summer I passed, but barely, with a grade of D.

I also had to make up Intermediate French and my teacher, a brother from one of our high schools in New England, taught several of us. In order to graduate, Catholic University mandated a foreign language examination at the end of the sophomore year and that test centered on French to English translation so our French courses emphasized this approach. Brother Aloysius tried to explain how the intricacies of French idioms could be expressed in English but realized I didn't render them as accurately as I should. At the end of the summer semester, the day before the final examination, he suggested I should visit him that evening so he could tutor me one last time.

The faculty lived apart from the scholastics on the second and third floor of the mansion that overlooked the parade grounds, a three story, one hundred ten room brick building, whose official name was Indian Neck Hall. Decorated by Commodore Bourne as lavishly as his gardens, the mansion showcased wealth.

I entered the front door into a spacious foyer where Persian rugs lined the parquet floor. Crystal chandeliers hung from the ceilings. Ten foot double doors made of oak with embedded stained glass led to a variety of sitting rooms adorned with marble and mahogany fireplaces. I walked up the oak staircase, down the carpeted corridor to Brother Aloysius's room and knocked. He answered and told me to come in. The large room was divided into a bedroom area with a bureau and highboy. A separate sitting room with a luxurious reading chair and an oak desk, hardly resembled the quarters of a brother with a vow of poverty. At the far end of the room the double window looked out onto the parade grounds; beyond, the water of the Great South Bay of the Long Island Sound shimmered in the dusk. I sensed immediately something unfamiliar about the room and about Brother Aloysius. On the lamp table next to the chair I saw a cocktail glass filled with ice. He picked up the glass, took a sip and then walked to a side table. He unscrewed the top of a bottle, walked back to the chair and refilled his glass. The bottle was Scotch, Brother Aloysius drank and, as I later learned, he fit the definition of a functioning alcoholic. He wasn't drunk, tipsy perhaps, a little slower than usual, but he started tutoring me immediately. I sat at the desk and he stood over me flipping through his copy of the textbook.

"Turn to this page," he said, as he pointed to the number in his book. "Translate the two paragraphs on the top of the page." He returned to his chair, continued sipping his scotch and reading his book while I started to translate. "Tell me when you're finished," he said.

While he read and replenished his glass, I translated for several minutes then showed him my work. He sighed.

"This is a very important essay," he said, then repeated it for emphasis. "Very important."

I nodded. He circled some parts of my translation and corrected my mistakes explaining the proper answer and continuing to insist that not only was the entire essay important, very important he repeated again, but I had translated each French phrase literally rather than understanding the idiomatic meaning in the French language. Nevertheless, he suggested that I might even try to memorize all these important paragraphs. I attempted translating several more sections and he corrected them until he ended our meeting when the bell for night prayer rang. I thanked him, left him alone to finish his Scotch and walked downstairs to the chapel. Brother Aloysius's admonitions rattled around my brain during night prayer. All I could remember was that everything he told me was important, very important, and I couldn't recall half of it. During night prayer I prayed for enlightenment asking God to infuse me with just enough knowledge to pass French.

The next morning he distributed the final exam. Immediately I recognized the essay I needed to translate; the same one I struggled with on the night before in his room. I'm sure he had already mimeographed the test the previous night when he tutored me to translate. I tried as hard as I could to repeat what he had told me, not to translate literally, and I did well enough, or maybe he had pity on me, to earn a C in Intermediate French.

The Brothers never considered alcoholism an institutional problem. They frowned more on brothers who smoked than those who imbibed. I don't remember any warnings about the problems of drinking, either physical or spiritual, but if the disease worsened to the point where a person became unaccountable, the brothers quietly arranged for the brother to be hospitalized and rehabilitated, although this assessment occurred rarely. Perhaps this laissez-faire attitude recognized that within any large group of people some will be alcoholics or perhaps, since a majority of brothers came from Irish families, the brothers merely tolerated the disease as a cultural trait. In many cases with alcoholics they only faced the disease when it affected their jobs, and, as their economic livelihood worsened, their families eventually gave up on them. An alcoholic brother always had a job in the classroom, the vow of poverty prevented him from actually being poor and the community where he lived wasn't going anywhere. The alcoholic brother always had support.

I took two other courses that summer: a general biology course for two credits—it didn't have a lab component—and Speech Education for Teachers. The speech education course concentrated on the techniques of using my voice in a classroom. I was taught pronunciation, enunciation and the importance of both. The brothers led the crusade for keeping the "t" silent in the word "often." My major problem involved modulating my voice and when I thought I was speaking in a normal tone others asked me to stop yelling. Had I been born in the 19th century I would have made a great circus barker.

One speech assignment involved composing questions worded in ways that, rather than confusing them, assisted them in ascertaining the correct answers. When asked, a question should be clearly constructed and spoken slowly. When questioning students, I learned how to stand or sit after I posed the question. I needed to remain silent and wait for a student response rather than blurt out the correct answer. I even learned how to ask a question as I stood in the doorway or looked out a window.

We examined gesturing in detail: how to point, how to use one hand rather than two and how to turn around. I learned how to use the pointer at the blackboard and how to tap it on the desk or even someone's shoulder for emphasis, all without speaking. One strategy I learned involved walking slowly to the side of the classroom and then drifting along the wall to the back and asking the question from there and say firmly to those students whose eyes followed me, "Don't look at me. The answer is written on the blackboard." Teaching from the back of the classroom always seemed to heighten the students' attention as if I was sneaking up on them.

Later, in some other pedagogical course, I read *An Actor Prepares* by Constantin Stanislavski and realized that what actors do on stage can be utilized in the classroom.[15] "Remember this," Stanislavski wrote, "All of our acts, even the simplest, which are so familiar to us in everyday life, become more strained when we appear behind the footlights." I substituted the phrase "in front of the classroom" for "behind the footlights" and tried to examine every movement I made in our practice classroom. Stanislavski continued; "That is why it is necessary to correct ourselves and learn again how to walk, move about, sit, or lie down." Later in my teaching career I think I shocked some of my students when, rather than bend, I knelt down on one knee at the blackboard and wrote something at the bottom of the board near the chalk ledge.

I delighted in Oakdale with its wide expanse of parade grounds, walking to chapel in the morning, engulfed by fog washing in from the Long Island Sound and being part of a larger community of Brothers. Having lived for two years among the same forty faces, I enjoyed meeting another hundred scholastics, the juniors and seniors. I knew many of them from my sophomore days in the Juniorate when they were juniors and seniors in high school. Now, as a sophomore in college, they would teach me again how to survive in an even more stringent academic environment.

Compared to the Novitiate with its regimen of prayer and spiritual reading and Hillside Hall with its even more arduous academic schedule—six courses totaling twenty college credits—I felt relaxed at Oakdale and ultra-relaxed on Wednesday afternoons. Brother Leo, attempting to find new meanings in common words, commented on the word recreation and explained that the word had two parts, "re" and "creation," and every Wednesday afternoon he suspended the serious side of the religious life and insisted our intellectual lives be recharged with play.

After lunch almost everyone stayed to clean up the refectory. Most cleared the tables, washed and dried the dishes and set the table with juice glasses and cereal bowls for the next meal—not dinner that evening—but breakfast the next morning. Supper would be on one of beaches farther out on Long Island. While most of the brothers cleared the dishes, others made hundreds of peanut butter and jelly sandwiches, stored coolers with hamburgers and hotdogs, potato and macaroni salads, coleslaw and mixed an apple, strawberry and grape juice concoction, called "bug juice," since it attracted hundreds of yellow jackets who swarmed around the lips of a half dozen ten gallon milk cans. We loaded the food and drink onto a truck along with picnic tables, bags of charcoal, volleyball and badminton nets. We returned to our rooms, changed into our bathing suits, packed towels, sandals, suntan lotion and a good novel, boarded a bus and headed east toward the beaches in the Hamptons.

When we arrived, about an hour later, we unloaded the truck, set up the picnic tables, started the portable grills and settled down for an afternoon at the beach. On my first trip to the beach I thought the ride to the Hamptons took excessively long and, except for the trips to and from Troy and learning how to drive the stick shift there, hadn't travelled outside a monastery in two years.

The last time I walked on the beach was the summer of 1958 when, on my final summer visit home, I stayed with my family on the Jersey shore. As I trudged over the dunes at the Hamptons and saw the Atlantic Ocean, I stood for several minutes marveling at how the ocean, for all its tides and swells, didn't appear changed in three years. During the summers I spent on the New Jersey shore I stood on the beach, looked straight out and imagined someone on a beach in Spain or Portugal looked back at me. Here on the southern shore of Long Island staring straight out meant south toward the beaches of Cuba or Haiti.

Besides a blanket and a book I brought my binoculars and wandered for miles searching for terns, sandpipers and gulls. The only person I missed was Brother Eulogius Austin who could have distinguished, at a hundred yards, how the wing patterns of the sanderling differed from those of the spotted sandpiper. Most brothers who expressed an interest in bird watching let their enthusiasm wane except for John Harrington and we would spend fifteen minutes watching one sandpiper race the waves back and forth on the beach as they searched for food in the sand.

About five o'clock the brothers who cooked checked the status of the charcoal, unpacked the coolers and started grilling. As six o'clock approached everyone gathered to eat. We sat on blankets, balanced our paper plates on our knees, stuffed our drinking glasses into the sand so they wouldn't tip over and, gluttony being encouraged by Brother Leo, ate as much as we wanted so we wouldn't have to take the food back to Oakdale.

After loading the tables back on the truck, Brother Leo gestured to us to form a circle. We stood three or four deep and he stepped into the middle and led us in night prayer. At the end we paused and one of the lead cantors intoned the first words of the Marian antiphon *Salve Regina.* We ended the day singing the simple Gregorian Chant version as dusk descended on the beach. One of the popular books for spiritual reading among the Brothers at that time was Rudolf Otto's *The Idea of the Holy* in which he popularized the word numinous, the experience of something totally other than oneself that can't be seen. I remember those evenings as the most intense experience I have ever had of God the Creator. If Brother Leo had said I could pitch a tent and stay the night I would never have left.

Chapter 16

Early one morning in late August 1961 I packed my duffel bag once again, loaded it on a truck and watched it pull away. I would see my belongings later that day in my assigned room at De La Salle College just outside of Washington, D.C., or so I thought.

After Morning Prayer and breakfast I performed my final manual labor assignment at Oakdale. I stripped my bed, swept and mopped the floor, then went downstairs to find my name on the bus list assignment. Our convoy of yellow buses pulled out of La Salle Military Academy and onto the Sunrise Highway and headed west. In the summer of 1961 Long Island had its numerous parkways: Wantagh, Meadowbrook, Cross Island and the Northern and Southern State and all of them prohibited buses and commercial vehicles. The Long Island Expressway wouldn't extend into Suffolk County until the mid 1960s so our route took us west into Queens and Brooklyn. I spent three summers at Oakdale. After the

Verrazano-Narrows Bridge was completed in 1964 I remember traveling that way on our return in the summer of 1964 but in August of 1961 we travelled on many local roads through Queens, downtown Brooklyn and through the Holland Tunnel into New Jersey.

We had hardly gone an hour when I felt extraordinarily tired. Even my anticipation at arriving in Washington couldn't keep me focused. Most of the brothers on the bus were engaged in conversations about what we sophomores should expect when we reached De La Salle College in Washington; what courses we would take and who are new teachers would be. Everyone exhibited excitement except me. All I wanted to do was close my eyes, so I moved to the back of the bus and spread myself out across an empty seat and went to sleep. I remember I woke up momentarily, noticed the oil refineries and realized I was on the New Jersey Turnpike but I couldn't stay awake. The next time I woke I realized the bus had stopped and everyone was getting off. We had arrived at the Scholasticate and I felt my enthusiasm would carry through my malady. I tried to stand but felt like I was wearing a heavy winter coat soaked with water. A brother must have encouraged me to get up and, when I said I couldn't, he summoned Brother Leo. Propped up in the back seat I answered questions as best I could. No, I didn't feel sick. No, I didn't have any aches or pains other than the feeling of total lightheadedness. I tried to walk up the aisle of the bus but my legs collapsed like a foal being born. A couple of brothers opened the emergency door at the rear of the bus and I was carried out of the bus like a piece of luggage.

I glanced quickly at the building, a long four storey brick structure with a grand stone staircase in the middle. It reminded me of Barrytown. Two brothers threw my arms over their shoulders and carried me up the front steps toward my assigned room on the top floor. Instead, Brother Leo instructed them to carry me to the infirmary, a small room with one bed and a private bath. Another brother brought me a change of clothing and my pajamas and despite having slept on the bus most of the day I slept the entire night.

Brother Leo awoke me the next morning offering me a glass of water and asking if I wanted to receive Holy Communion. I said yes and he left me for a moment. I felt better and could stand but I was afraid of trying to walk. Gliding along a wall I looked out the door into an empty corridor I didn't recognize. Several minutes later I heard sacristy bells ringing. Two brothers wearing white surplices and holding lighted candles approached the door. They entered the infirmary and a priest, wearing a purple stole and holding a small host box, followed them. He opened the box, recited a collect and offered me communion. I stuck out my tongue and swallowed the host. It was the first food I'd eaten in twenty-four hours, unleavened bread never tasted so good, although technically it wasn't food.

Later, I learned rumors had circulated that, not only had I received Holy Communion that morning, but also the last rites before death, the sacrament of Extreme Unction. No one in the

Scholasticate could remember the last time communion had been brought to the sick.

After a small breakfast I felt better and later in the morning a doctor arrived to examine me. After looking up my nose and down my throat, taking my temperature and pulse and listening to my lungs with his stethoscope he mysteriously concluded that my ailment involved a potassium deficiency and that I should start immediately on a special diet.

I had never heard of such a diagnosis except my grandmother's regular habit of taking spoonfuls of Geritol to ward off the dreaded disease of iron deficiency anemia. As a child I remember the advertisement that claimed a spoonful of Geritol contained "twice the amount of iron as a pound of calf's liver" which never endeared me to the product. Once a week growing up my mother fried up slices of liver and attempted to make the meat palpable by dressing it with bacon strips oozing fat.

My new diet contained foods loaded with potassium and Brother Leo granted permission for me to snack between meals. I could eat dates, bananas, apricots and peanuts as much as I wanted until I was strong enough and gained weight. Brother Leo, now concerned not only with my spiritual health but about my physical well-being—I had sprouted to 6' 2" but weighed only 150 pounds—also allowed me to make a snack after night prayer. While the other brothers went to their rooms I walked to the kitchen and rustled up a malted milkshake: several scoops of ice cream, whole milk, chocolate syrup, a banana, several scoops of malt and two raw eggs. I dumped the ingredients into a blender and sat in the refectory each evening drinking a quart of this concoction. Within two weeks, aided by my nightly allowance of ice cream fat, I regained my strength along with an extra ten pounds and Brother Leo curtained my need for night-time nourishment. This was Brother Leo's theory of putting on weight and he was right; eat, eat a lot, and eat a lot of fat.

He was universally liked, the type of person you might say didn't have a bad bone in his body but one time his anger got a hold on him. Some brother or perhaps several brothers had done something—I don't remember the particulars— that piqued him immensely. It was a Sunday and periodically on some Sundays evenings all the brothers gathered in the narrow recreation room on the bottom floor of the Scholasticate to view a movie.

The third and fourth floors were divided into bedrooms, baths and showers, the second floor was divided into the common room, classrooms and several smaller rooms dedicated to specific activities. There were two music rooms with strict rules for what type of music could be played. One was the "classical" music room where Mozart, Beethoven or Brahms could be heard while people in the other room would listen to Broadway show tunes. The bottom floor, however, was open, like a gigantic loft apartment. Almost the whole floor was dedicated to recreation. There were pool tables, ping-pong tables and sofas for just lounging around. In the corner a television, rarely watched, hung from the ceiling. Brothers were allowed to talk to each other in the recreation room. Brothers went to the recreation room to discuss some academic matter or just to converse.

On that particular Sunday evening the schedule included a movie to be shown in the recreation room about a half hour after supper. Instead, Brother Leo, at the end of supper, announced that in a half hour, instead of congregating in the recreation room, we were all to go to our desks in the common room. There, he announced, that our collective punishment for the transgressions of the few, would be two extra hours of study rather than seeing the film. And, unlike watching a movie, silence should be strictly observed until night prayer. The denial of a movie because of the actions of a few violated our sense of fairness. Why should the entire Scholasticate be punished when most of us were innocent? We looked at each other in disbelief at the injustice of it all and, while we were not happy with whoever got us into this predicament, we all sensed that Brother Leo had lost his sense of proportional punishment.

With 125 brothers sitting around in seething silence, there was bound to be an act of recrimination. It wasn't long before our form of retaliation became clear. The next event would be night prayer and someone—again I plead ignorance as to who—devised a plot to get even with Brother Leo. During night prayer we would protest anonymously as a group.

There are several sections of night prayer: examination of conscience, a collect, and a short litany. Toward the end of night prayer the entire congregation recites the hymn *Te Lucis*, the

188

traditional hymn at Compline. The hymn asks God to preserve us chastely through the night and to deny the devil access to our minds and hearts. One of the verses reads as follows.

> Far off let idle visions fly
> No phantom of the night molest
> Curb thou our raging enemy
> That we in chaste repose may rest.

When referring to Brother Leo informally it was customary to call him by his nickname. His family name was "Kirby" and from this name he acquired the nickname "Kirb." He was well aware that this is what we all called him when he wasn't present. Someone noticed that his nickname and the first word of the third line in that night prayer, "curb," were pronounced the same way and suggested that instead of the customary recitation of the entire line without any breaks that we all pause after the word "curb" as if there was a double dash. Now the line would be recited "Curb—thou our raging enemy." The plan for retribution circulated through the common room, one brother whispering the plan to the next. Brother Leo sitting at his desk in the front of the common room read calmly and didn't look at us intently. He may have had second thoughts. The air of the common room reeked of recrimination.

We whispered the plan from one desk to another and as it spread we enjoyed our deviousness as much as we might have enjoyed the movie. The only question remaining was how many of us would dare recite the verse differently. If only one or two did it, it would be obvious who they were. If several dozen chimed in it would be harder to tell who ruined the cadence of that line in the hymn.

I approached night prayer approached with trepidation; on one hand I thought Brother Leo reacted too drastically. On the other hand I was hardly the rebel. When the time came to recite the verse several dozen brothers recited the line with the pause and when they paused the remainder of the line stood out very clearly-"Curb—thou our raging enemy." The brothers who sat in the back of the chapel reported later, that the faculty, who sat in the last two pews, were startled at the dissonance. They, of course, were totally unaware of the plot. At we filed out of the chapel at the end of night prayer it was unusual to see so many brothers smiling. Nothing ever came of the incident and Brother Leo never again deprived us of a movie on Sunday evening.

My sophomore year proved uneventful. My course load of twenty credits included Introduction to French Literature in the first semester which I passed, if only with a grade of D, and with a grade of C in the second semester. I found it hard to believe I could get better. That second semester was the first semester in college I didn't get a grade of D or F. I managed to get a C in Calculus II and a B in Calculus III. I thought I was on my way to academic honors. How wrong I was.

The courses during the sophomore year were all held at De La Salle College and not Catholic University of America. I would not attend classes there until my junior year. I was one of the few chosen to major in Physics since our high schools needed physics teachers and I would be groomed to teach the subject.

During the first semester in the General College Physics course I got a grade of C and did slightly better the second semester with a grade of B. I didn't think about it then but it should have been a warning. The grade for this course should have been an A because the Physics courses during my junior and senior year would not only be difficult, they would be on an entirely different level. I had no idea what I was getting into.

Chapter 17

I enjoyed my sophomore year in Washington—I didn't fail anything. Although enrolled as a student of the Catholic University of America, I attended all my courses at De La Salle College and carried a load of twenty credits. My instructors also attended Catholic University where they studied for their doctorates. Two of my teachers had taught me before in the Juniorate and they knew my capabilities or lack thereof. Brother Bernard enjoyed teaching French and I still hated learning it. I received a grade of D in the fall but managed inexplicably to raise my grade to C in the spring. Brother Gerard taught Calculus as well as he had taught me Geometry in the sophomore year in the Juniorate. I earned my best grades in Religion and Philosophy and should have realized my best prospect in college would have been in the arts and not the sciences.

At Oakdale in the summer between my sophomore and junior years I rejoiced that I could enroll in normal summer courses rather than repeating failed courses and I imagined what the daily routine of a high school teacher might be. I would major in Physics and teach it but every brother also taught a religion class so most summer courses at Oakdale included one in theology. In the course, "Bible and Modern Criticism" I read Rudolf Bultmann's *Form Criticism* which explained how the gospels emerged from an oral tradition. Religion classes in the Juniorate rarely ventured into a historical examination of the synoptic gospels and instead concentrated on how God directed their written form. God inspired the writing and I envisioned a divine editor dictating the words verbatim. I wondered about the inherent problem of scripture's origin. Since the gospels of Matthew and Luke were most likely written in Aramaic, their translation into Greek, then into Latin and finally English guaranteed problems in meaning and interpretation. It bothered me than verse 2 from chapter 4 of John's gospel had certainly been translated incorrectly. "In my father's house there are many mansions." While I don't read Greek I'd bet the English word "mansions" should have been rendered "rooms." Catholic tradition belittled such concern. I remember being taught that even St. Jerome who translated the scriptures from Greek to Latin got entwined in the theory of divine inspiration—God, the divine editor, inspired his translation. Theology courses at Oakdale involved a mountain of unlearning.

The curriculum included another theology course, "Catechesis and Kerygma" where the latest in theological studies extended beyond traditional catholic dogma. I piled books high on my desk: Martin Buber's *I and Thou*, a Jewish philosopher's search for God and Paul Tillich's *The Courage to Be* proved challenging. Reading Hans Küng, a liberal catholic theologian, tested a few of my fundamental convictions about Roman Catholicism especially his questioning of the infallibility of the Pope. The Christian Brothers were not conservative Catholics.

I first attended courses at The Catholic University of America during the fall semester of my junior year, 1962. I had visited the campus several times during my sophomore year, mostly at nights to listen to lectures sponsored by the philosophy or religious education departments. On weekends the Speech and Drama Department, under the direction of Father Gilbert Harke, presented a Shakespearian comedy. Father Hartke, a Dominican priest, founded the Speech and Drama Department at Catholic University and singlehandedly raised, not only the student's awareness of the genius of Shakespeare, but that of the extended Washington, D.C. community. Father Hartke, dedicated to making the drama department known nationally, evolved into the man about town, a priest bon vivant in Washington as he plied the social and political circles of the Washington elite to raise funds for a modern theater to replace the ramshackle building on the edge of the campus. He increased his influence among the powerful so much that *Fortune* named him one of the most powerful men in Washington in 1981.

As the theater majors fleshed out the antics and frolics of Shakespeare's comic characters with a vaudevillian interpretation, the audience reacted with gusto: laughing out loud, guffawing and foot stomping often made the dialogue impossible to hear. I realized that viewing a performance of a Shakespeare comedy and reading the play were two different experiences. The last time I had witnessed a play being acted occurred in the Juniorate, the night I watched Hamlet on television after lights out.

The fall schedule of my junior year included two courses in Physics major. Had I paid more attention to the course numbers, I would have realized sooner what degree of anguish awaited me. While the religious education and philosophy courses had traditional course numbers in the 200s and 300s, the two physics courses had numbers in the 500s. Although I didn't realize it at the time, Catholic University didn't have a sufficient number of students majoring in physics to support both an undergraduate and graduate program. Intermediate Electricity and Magnetism (PHYS503) was the first course in the master's degree program and that's the way the instructor taught it, as if most of the curriculum was a review of a course called *Introductory* Electricity and Magnetism. Its companion course, Theoretical Mechanics (PHYS509) demanded even more. As if two graduate physics courses weren't enough, one of the required mathematics mathematical courses, Vectors and Matrices (MATH571), was also a graduate course. The required textbook for the other mathematics course, Differential Equations, had been translated from its Russian edition but the only English I remember in the text were short sentences like "It is easily seen that..." and "It logically follows that..." which connected one unintelligible differential equation to another. I studied these "easily seen" progressions and discovered that the transition from an initial form of the equation to the conclusion required a dozen more stages not mentioned in the text. I studied for hours and only moved three or four pages forward in the textbook.

I spent the majority of my day attending classes, studying and, when not engaged in academic activities, attended chapel exercises for morning, mid-day and evening prayer. If I read anything other than a textbook it was a spiritual reading book. An influential Roman Catholic author of that time was Thomas Merton and one of his popular books was *No Man Is An Island*. He derived the title from a poem of John Donne with the same name. I could hardly look at the cover page of this book; I felt alone. No other brothers majored in Physics; I studied alone. My superiors frowned upon fraternizing with classmates who weren't a member of a religious order. Toward the end of the semester when I attended class I thought the instructors spoke a foreign language. I sunk slowly in academic quicksand.

At the end of the semester Brother Leo called me into his office and handed me my official report card which bared the bad news. Not only had I failed Electricity and Magnetism but also Theoretical Mechanics. My grade point average for the semester plummeted to 1.26 and, if I had been an ordinary student, I would have been expelled, not only from the Physics Department, but the university itself as being unfit college material. But Brother Leo had influence and the university allowed me to attend classes during the spring semester. During the spring I could take my time to investigate another major. I struggled to accept the fact that I would not be graduating with my class.

I think it came as a surprise to Brother Leo that I chose to continue majoring in physics and would repeat the courses in the fall semester of 1963 but he did not question my decision. I was angry with myself for failing courses in the first place and determined that I would be successful; I did not surrender easily. I wondered if he admired my steadfastness or pitied my stubbornness. Only a handful of major decisions I made in my life proved imprudent and continuing to major in physics topped the list. I should have followed the advice attributed to W. C. Fields. "If at first you don't succeed, try, try again—then quit. There's no use being a damn fool about it."

Fortunately that next year four other brothers also majored in physics and another brother majored in Electrical Engineering. I ingratiated myself, studied with them, asked innumerable questions and followed whatever advice they gave me about passing these physics courses. Many years later at reunions I laughed when they admitted they endured their own struggles with the curriculum. At the time I thought it proved so easy for them.

During the autumn of 1963, events occurred that influenced me immensely. Pope John Paul XXIII had died the previous June. While we heard few details about the first session of the Second Vatican Council, speculation circulated that Pope Paul VI would curtail, if not cancel, the second session of the council. He didn't. During the next decade, John Paul XXIII's metaphor of opening the windows of Roman Catholicism to let in fresh air of modern thought had unintended consequences. Roman Catholics started jumping out those windows.

The second event occurred on Friday, November 22, 1963. I waited on the library steps of Catholic University for the noon bus to take me back to De La Salle College. The bus was late and when it arrived the driver informed us that President Kennedy had been assassinated in Dallas, Texas. I am one of the generation who remembers exactly where I stood the moment I heard the news.

Since Thanksgiving would be on the next Thursday, the university cancelled the classes for Monday, Tuesday and Wednesday. I vacillated between watching the memorial services unfolding that weekend on TV and returning to my room and studying. The president would be waked, eulogized and buried but soon after I would have to pass my final exams in my physics courses.

Some brothers drove downtown to the capitol building and joined the throngs of mourners filing through the rotunda. I stayed at the Scholasticate and studied. I wondered about Brother Albinus of Mary whose enthusiasm for the nomination and election of John Kennedy and what great deeds he would do was now entirely shattered.

At the beginning of 1964 Brother Bertrand Leo assumed the office of Visitor of the New York District and Brother Augustine Loes replaced him as Director of the Scholasticate. In his *Concise History of the New York District* Brother Luke

Salm, a theology professor at Manhattan College in the Bronx noted this transition of authority and parenthetically remarked that in the Scholasticate "the winds of change stirred by Vatican II, which was still in session, were blowing strong."[16] None of us realized it then but the Second Vatican Council and the assassination of the president would alter the psyche of most American Catholics, including the Brothers.

While most everyone's world that winter was cloaked in sadness my attitude brightened—I didn't fail any courses. I earned a grade of C in Intermediate Electricity and Magnetism, a grade of B in Physical Chemistry and squeaked out a D in Theoretical Mechanics. I abandoned all illusions of a storied academic career and muddled through the next three semesters with consistent C grades in all my physics courses except for a grade of D in optics. I admired a grade of D—it wasn't an F—and I trudged toward my physics teaching career.

I approached the end of the spring semester of 1964 with a touch of melancholy. My friends would be graduated and receive their first teaching assignment while I had another year of study.

On Monday morning June 1, 1964 Brother Augustine called me into his office. He had replaced Brother Leo as Director of the Scholasticate. I did not know him well and his solemn demeanor contrasted against Brother Leo's bubbly personality. At first I feared I had miscalculated my grades and he would inform me that I had failed another physics course. I would be sentenced to two more years of imprisonment in Washington rather than one.

He wore his most somber face but got right to the point. That morning he had received a phone call. My anxiety soared. I imagined his conversation with the chairman of the physics department discussing my incompetency. The physics faculty had finally decided that my pitiable performance had disparaged the reputation of the physics department and they could endure me no longer. I steeled myself.

Instead, Brother Augustine told me my mother had called. My father had died of a heart attack that morning in the bathroom as he took a shower before going to work. I was shocked more than saddened and realized how distant I had become from my own parents. It had been eight years since I had left home at the age of fifteen and for the last four years I had only been home once. During those eight years I had no real relationship with my father other than the letters he sent periodically with details of life back in the Bronx that I had little interest in. One of the issues with the brothers concerned those who might not fulfill their vocation because they missed their family. In my case the brothers succeeded admirably; I was quite detached. In the eighth chapter of the gospel of Matthew there is a story about a disciple wishing to follow Jesus more thoroughly but asks that he be allowed to go home to bury his father. Jesus answers, "Follow me and leave the dead to bury their own dead." In lectures the brothers quoted this verse to impress upon us the idea that persevering in our vocation trumped loyalty to family. I embraced this advice wholeheartedly and had more affection for the brothers in the Scholasticate than I did for my own parents. When I relate the story of my early life and leaving home permanently at the age of fifteen I am asked why I ever considered such a decision or how callous I must have been or maybe I was an exceptionally naïve boy hoodwinked by religious hocus-pocus.

Now I understand I left home to get away from my parents although this conviction was not conscious at the time. No life-changing decision, of course, can be traced to a unique cause but I am sure that my desire to separate myself from my parents represented a substantial portion of my decision to leave home. Somewhere in my psyche the memory of getting spanked resided and, as a child, I tried to run away into the bedroom but as a teenager I could escape much farther and pretend I had a religious calling.

Brother Augustine asked me if there was anything he could do for me at that moment; it was the kind of question one should never ask in a moment of apprehension. I can't remember any other brother going home to attend a funeral of a non-relative. I doubt it ever happened. When my grandmother died in December, 1962 I never even thought to ask if I might attend the funeral. When I asked Brother Augustine if three of my friends could attend the requiem mass he first reacted nonplused but after a moment replied that he would consider it. I don't recall how many brothers attended my father's funeral from St. John's Church in Kingsbridge but there were enough of them in their black suits and robe to be noticed: Brother Augustine Leo accompanied by my three friends and several brothers who taught at St. John's School. As I sat in the pew, flanked by two families—my natural family and the Brothers of the Christian Schools—I had more affection for the latter than the former.

In my last year at Catholic University one hurdle remained—passing a three-day comprehensive examination in my major. From 9 to 5 on each of the three days I had to answer questions I hadn't thought about for a year or two, plus worry about other subjects a faculty member of the physics department might want to include on the exam. Even for the other brothers who had cruised through the curriculum, this task proved daunting. We organized study groups, solved problems on our own, lectured to each other and tried to anticipate what questions might be asked. I poured over previous comprehensive exams as if trying to decipher the Rosetta Stone.

One brother helped me a lot. Brother John displayed such intelligence and talent that he majored in Electrical Engineering. There wasn't a physics problem he couldn't crack. As he explained which theories to employ and how to set up the equations, I thought he demonstrated magic tricks with cards. He never lost his patience even when he had to explain the solutions a second and third time. Physics ran in his DNA. Even his last name, Ott, looked and sounded like a physical quantity: amp, ohm, watt and Ott.

Finally, as the three-day exam approached, I could comprehend no more and decided to memorize complete answers to questions I thought might be asked. Luckily that decision proved wise. On the third day of the exam a question jumped off the page. I had memorized an answer to a question asking for the organization of the electro-magnetic spectrum and I wrote frenetically every detail about wavelengths and frequencies I could recall even illustrating my essay with diagrams using colored pencils. My wariness about failing diminished—the journeyman physics major had hit a homerun in the bottom of the ninth—and I anticipated the results of the comprehensive examination. By the end of May the physics department would send me a postcard with one letter on the blank side: A, B, C or F. If I received an F, I would have to repeat the senior year over again. As I left the examination room I stopped, envisioned the electromagnetic spectrum and panicked. I had written a detailed and exhaustive explanation of the electro-magnetic spectrum but made an egregious error—I had constructed the entire spectrum backwards. My analysis placed radio waves at the short frequency of the spectrum and radiation at the long end. This error, so fundamentally flawed, doomed me; I had the universe backwards and inside out.

The postcard arrived and on the back someone had written the letter C. I was positive this was an error but the error stood. I imagined the physics professors pondering my fate, shaking their heads at my ineptitude, and I think they just wanted to get rid of me. On the bottom of the last page of my transcript there is an entry for the result of the comprehensive exam. Mine says Physics and then the result written in quotation marks, "C." I wondered if they were trying to tell me something.

On June 6, 1965 I was graduated with the degree *Baccalaureatus Artium*. Father Hartke, influential in Washington circles, asked President Johnson to give the graduation speech and maneuvering around the campus that morning resembled searches at airport gates today. The secret service took no chances when the president appeared in public.

His commencement address sounded quite like a Catholic sermon at Sunday mass: excessive ideas couched in a rambling presentation, unrelated quotations from a founding father (Jefferson) and a dead predecessor (Kennedy), punctuated by pithy observations followed by the obligatory pauses for applause. He managed to string together references to the Chaldeans, the 21st anniversary of D-Day, Pope John XXIII and Major White, an astronaut.

He ended the speech paraphrasing the Taoist proverb of Lao-tzu that every journey begins with a first step and immediately took his own advice and exited hurriedly down the main aisle, flanked by the secret service, like he had to go to the bathroom. My sister sat on an aisle seat and as the president passed she offered her hand and he shook it briefly.

Over my five years in college I logged 222 credits and my final GPA was 2.4772. To my amazement I was ranked 181 out of 258 graduates and found it astonishing that 77 students were ranked below me. Although the grades don't suggest it, I believe I had an extraordinary education. I loved all my learning in philosophy, theology, chemistry, mathematics, literature, music, and psychology. I could finally admit I hated physics but for the next two years I would teach it and despise it all the more.

Chapter 18

After graduation I relaxed. No physics problems to solve, no preparation for tests and no uncertainty about failing. I resolved to postpone any further education as long as possible although I know the brothers expected me to attend graduate school. During the summer of 1965 I took one more course but this time I would be in the front of the classroom not in one of the seats.

The course title was Practice Teaching in Junior High School (EDUC391), a methodology course as it was known. Instead of traveling to Oakdale in the summer of 1965, I spent July and August at La Salle Academy on 2nd Street in New York City and taught two sections of Introductory Algebra to students who had failed it during the school year. They had my unadulterated sympathy—I knew how they felt.

Each morning Brother Andrew, my mentor, sat in the back of the classroom taking notes about my classroom deportment; his job—to teach me how to teach. During the break between sections he conferred with me and provided pointers on teaching the material in the second class. At times when my presentation faltered he would walk to the front of the class and demonstrate it correctly. The students appeared bemused at his teaching as he interspersed advice to me while instructing them. He knew all the students so I experienced no discipline problems; he had failed many of them during the spring semester. His practical suggestions included how to stand at a blackboard (don't block its view when you're writing), move left to right across the blackboard (refer back to what I had already written), before erasing the board ask if any student still needs to copy notes and never ever teach while you're sitting down.

Over my forty-five years of teaching I've perfected my pedagogical skills and continue to model my presentations by adopting the acting theories of Constantin Stanislavski. In his book *An Actor Prepares* Stanislavski note that when a person enters a stage all the most ordinary movements are strained. He says "It is necessary to correct ourselves and learn again how to walk, move about, sit or lie down. It is essential to re-educate ourselves to look and see, on the stage, to listen and to hear."[17] I substituted the word "classroom" for stage but often thought of the classroom as stage and adopted many specific behaviors when I taught. I used the entire room to teach making mental notes to myself. Don't just stand up in the front of the blackboard. Move around the classroom, up and down the aisles, stand in the back, and ask questions from the back of the classroom where the students will only hear your voice and hearing only your voice will pay closer attention. I envisioned Brother Eugene back in my seventh grade classroom. That's exactly what he did. Brother Gerald in Geometry stood over my desk, peered over my shoulder and commented on how to improve my note-taking.

Another suggestion I received concerned asking the class a question. Always pose the question first then ask for a specific student to answer it. If you select a particular student before asking the question then the other students tend to relax since they realized they wouldn't be called on. And when I did call upon a specific student I was not to point at him with my palm turned down and a hand clenched in a fist. This was an accusatory gesture. Instead, when I called upon a student I should extend my right hand with my palm up in a non-threatening gesture of invitation.

A teaching adage went like this: students hear fifty percent of what you say, understand fifty percent of what they hear and remember fifty percent of what they understand. Hence, every major point of a lesson must be repeated at least twice but in a different way so my teaching would not turn boring.

And lastly, act sternly, speak seriously, enunciate precisely and don't smile in class 'til Christmas.

Toward the middle of August, Brother Andrew often replaced me at the front of the class as the end of the course approached. While he deemed my teaching adequate, the problem for him concerned the students passing the Regents Exam of New York State. They were here precisely because they had failed that exam the previous June. In the last week of class he drilled them unmercifully in the techniques of Regents test taking. Each day the students worked on a section from a previous year's exam and scored it immediately to identify their weaknesses. Brother Andrew assigned another practice test as their homework. He, like many of the brothers, had scant regard for the test itself and even less respect for the state government who mandated it as a requirement for a Regents diploma in New York State. I watched from the back of the classroom as he guided them through the pitfalls of the examination as if leading them through a minefield.

"Don't touch that problem," he cautioned one student. "You have no idea what it's about. Cross it out; don't even read it. Many students received the same advice—avoid the dreaded "word" problems.

Brother Andrew taught me how to correct the tests but I also had to learn how to get the students through. The Algebra Regents had two parts. The first part contained thirty questions to which there was only one correct answer for each question. That section of the exam provided no leeway: each question was worth two points, with no partial credit, for a total of sixty points. After correcting the first part of each exam I subtracted the student's score from sixty-five. That value guided me as I corrected part two of the exam. In order for the student to pass the exam, the combined score for both parts of the exam had to equal sixty-five or greater. Rather than correct the second part of the exam I scanned the student's answers trying to find enough points by partial credit for the student to pass. Once I found enough valid points I could correct the exam anyway I wanted. If possible, calculate a grade of 67 or 68 in the event that the State Department of Education should review the exams and question some of my corrections.

The summer course ended; no readings, no reports, no papers, and no tests. Brother Andrew submitted his evaluation to Catholic University. I earned a grade of B. How he arrived at this I have no idea.

I received my teaching assignment for the school year 1965-1966; Queen of Peace High School in North Arlington, New Jersey. I arrived several days before school started and was startled at the lackadaisical attitude toward the religious life. As I unpacked I realized my bedroom contained a bed, bureau, and nightstand but also a chair, desk and bookcases. The brothers' house had no common room. A brother not only slept in his bedrooms but used it like an office: preparing lessons, correcting papers, and listening to the radio. Each bedroom also had a small sink and medicine cabinet in one corner of the room. The brothers' residence felt more like a fraternity house than a religious community. This living configuration surprised me for in my nine years in the houses of formation (Juniorate, Novitiate and Scholasticate) the monastic rule forbade being in the bedroom for any other reason than for sleeping or changing clothes. In the years of formation the rule also called for silence in the bedroom. Here, two or three brothers would congregate in a bedroom, pulling up chairs or sitting on the bed and chatted as if at a picnic.

The next morning brought more revelations. I had to set my alarm so I would wake at 6 A.M. No general bell would ring. I showered, shaved and put on my religious habit. Morning Prayer started at 6:30 and I arrived five minutes early. Only two of the dozen brothers knelt in the pews; Brother Patrick, the Brother Director, and Brother Robert, the taciturn brother who had taught me in St. Bernard's High School ten years earlier. I assumed the others would arrive just as Morning Prayer started but only two or three others showed up. Brother Patrick intoned the opening prayer and the responses of the brothers sounded halfhearted. They mumbled their way through the prayers as if it were a penance after confession. After Morning Prayer Brother Patrick read several verses of a scriptural reading then we knelt or sat in silence, presumably this was meditation time, until one of the priests from the parish arrived to say mass. The responses at mass sounded just as dreary as Morning Prayer and during my two years there we only sang hymns on major feasts. On Sundays we walked across the street to the church to attend Mass and every brother attended to avoid giving scandal about missing mass on Sunday. The liturgy that had been an essential part of my spiritual life felt listless and lethargic. The brothers navigated daily mass like robots.

I finally realized that two communities existed simultaneously—the religious community in which many of spiritual practices I experienced in formation disappeared and the school community that dominated most of my time.

One flaw existed in the hierarchy of the Christian Brothers. One person could not act as the principal of the school and the Brother Director of the community. Most of principals were chosen for their administrative abilities and had little expertise and no inclination to be a spiritual director. The principals ran the schools well but ignored the role of community director. Teaching assumed a paramount role; spirituality declined. My spiritual life became unmoored.

When I arrived, Queen of Peace High School existed as a co-institutional school, rather than a co-educational school, and boys on the second floor of the school were separated from girls on the first floor. The Sisters of St. Joseph of Chestnut Hill, Pennsylvania started the school in 1930. They taught both the boys and the girls until the Christian Brothers arrived in 1960. The school was divided into a boys' department and a girls' department with separate principals and faculty. Integration only occurred at football or basketball games, at dances on Saturday nights in the gym and with the publication of the school yearbook where the photographs of the graduates were listed in alphabetical order.

The sisters maintained a dress policy for the girls: a white blouse with a round collar underneath a blue neck-to-below-the-knee skirt with a QP coat of arms on the left shoulder. While no uniform dress code existed for the boys, they wore white shirts, solid colored ties and sport coats.

My schedule included one Religion course, two Introductory Algebras, one Intermediate Algebra and an honors Physics course. The school day started with each brother teaching a Religion class to his homeroom. I taught one of the two new freshman classes during the first period and then after a brief break switched gears and taught them Introductory Algebra in the second period. The custom at Queen of Peace dictated that many of the teachers move from one classroom to another while the majority of students remained in the same classroom when that was possible. The students only moved when the schedule included a science lab or when they had lunch.

I enjoyed teaching Religion and Mathematics but dreaded my last class of the day—Honors Physics. Someone had already selected the textbook for the course, *PSSC Physics* (Physical Science Study Committee), a heavy tome that incorporated concepts from Newton to Einstein. A group at MIT developed the course in 1956 for bright students and the seniors enrolled in my class quickly demonstrated their intelligence. My minimal command of the curriculum dictated I stay at least one chapter ahead of what I taught. Fortunately, the teacher guides included the solutions to all the problems I assigned for homework so I wouldn't have to solve them myself. One or two of the brighter students might have taught the course more competently than I did.

In a yearbook photograph one of my physics students who asked many questions is standing at the blackboard with the Physics textbook in his one hand and pointing to the blackboard with the other. I am sitting in the front seat. The caption reads, "For the first time this year everyone is where he belongs." I fooled no one.

Once a week the class moved to the physics lab where the students, using a detailed lab manual supplied by the publisher, tried to prove the acceleration due to gravity was 9.8 meters per second squared or compute the coefficient of friction for common substances. At least I didn't have to prepare a lecture. I muddled through without the torture of preparing the students for a Regents exam since New Jersey didn't require them.

When the school day ended at 3 P.M., I returned to the Brothers' house and changed into recreational clothes. Each brother coordinated an after-school activity: football moderator, drama club advisor or a coach, believing that some students would understand the altruistic life we led as religious and decide to join us—a few of them would have a vocation. During these years the Christian Brothers closed some elementary schools and opened new high schools or assumed control of those that already existed. They concluded that the fertile ground of Northern New Jersey as best suited to attract high school graduates to the religious life. The Brothers arrived at Queen of Peace High School in 1960, took over St. Joseph's High School in West New York, New Jersey, closed De La Salle Institute on 74th Street in Manhattan and opened up Christian Brothers Academy in Lincroft, New Jersey. Closing De La Salle institute rattled some of the older brothers. The school origins dated back to 1842 and it had been at its 74th Street location since 1924. In their view tradition didn't count for much anymore.

Brother Patrick assigned me to assist Brother Maurice as the track coach. I knew little about track and delved into reading textbooks about the sport and following Brother Maurice's advice. My own experience came in the Juniorate when I often ran cross country just for the fun of it. I could throw off my anxiety and frustration and after running could only feel the emotion of exhaustion. Brother Maurice gave me my equipment: a whistle, clipboard, hat and a school wind breaker with the inscription "coach" and informed me I was the official freshman track coach.

Track teams operated for the entire school year: cross-country in the fall, indoor track in the winter and outdoor track in the spring so for ten months I was busy every afternoon. When the team travelled to meets at other schools or regional events I often missed dinner. When I returned I heated some leftovers and ate alone in the dining room.

The students who joined the team understood that as long as they came to practice they could be on the team. Unlike football and basketball where only the best are selected and the rest are cut, the track team accepted all who could don a pair of shorts and sneakers and run for two hours around the track. Their daily reward included stomach cramps, shin splints and foot blisters but the track community kept the medal industry alive. At each dual meet, when two schools competed against each other, Brother Maurice believed that everyone who earned a point during the meet should receive a medal or a ribbon. However, some boys who possessed so little athletic talent often went without this reward. For these boys I set individual goals. If you ran the half-mile event in one meet in a time of 3:30 (a very slow time) your goal was to take a least one second off that time and at the next meet run the event in 3:29.

I remember one boy in particular. Most of the boys called each other by their first names or some nickname: Dan, Joey, Doug or Shep. This particular boy, however, always went by his last name, Hennessey. He was in my homeroom so I taught him religion and algebra and knew him well; shy, bright and very determined. He was also short and when he ran his stride hardly put one foot in front of the other. He elected to run the two mile event since it was less embarrassing to finish ten minutes behind everyone else rather than seventy yards back in a hundred yard dash. It pained me to watch him. Rather than running the two mile he slugged through it. Since the two mile event occurred last at meets, Hennessey could take his time finishing, but each time he ran he finished and I'd report his progress, two seconds faster than last week. It wasn't much but it was improvement and I could always count on Hennessey to finish despite how much he hurt.

At one meet involving three schools Brother Maurice and I planned how to accumulate the most points in order to win the meet. When meets involved three or more schools, points were awarded from first to fifth place (five points for the winner, four points to second place and so on). Runners were restricted to two track events and one field event (javelin, high jump, shot put and the like) so we had to carefully plan our entries so our best athletes would win. Hennessey, of course, would run the two mile.

During the meet my student manager kept me informed of the total score as each event reported its results to the official referee. As the end of the meet approached I knew from watching the events that the score would be close. When the two mile started I noticed there were only six runners in the event. If Hennessey could manage to finish fifth he would earn his first point in a meet and his first ribbon. As the race progressed its outcome was hardly in doubt. The two best runners set a quick pace and quickly separated themselves from the pack. It wasn't long before they lapped Hennessey. I asked my manager to total up the score based on my anticipated order of finish for the two mile and tell me who would win the meet. He made a quick calculation and then looked at me strangely. I asked him, "What's was the matter?" I thought he might have tallied the score incorrectly. He told me that if Hennessey finished fifth we'd win the meet by one point. If he didn't we'd lose by one point. The score was closer than I thought.

It didn't take long for my manager to tell the rest of the team. As Hennessey plodded through the first mile he had more on his shoulders than he realized. He was in sixth place but only by about ten yards. Accustomed to being ignored when he ran, Hennessey at first didn't understand all the fuss as his teammates ran alongside him on the inner track urging him to run faster and get into fifth place. The runner in front of Hennessey wasn't much better than he was so the fifth would go to the runner who wanted it the most. As Hennessey pulled closer and then passed the runner and into fifth place, his teammates cheered. Buoyed by the adulation, he started running faster and unless Hennessey fell down or stopped running we would win. As he crossed the finish line I thought his teammates might break his back as they slapped him repeatedly.

In the locker room, as he looked at his fifth place ribbon, I told him he had shaved eleven seconds off his best time. He never ran faster again.

Chapter 19

During my two years at Queen of Peace High School the intensity of my religious life waned. I started missing religious exercises. Many days only three of us attended morning prayer: Brother Patrick, the Director of the community, Brother Robert and me. Soon only two attended.

During the time for evening prayer, I remained at school with the track team. I walked the aisles of the locker room shooing tardy students out before locking up. Brother Maurice, one of the English teachers, taught me the details of managing of a high school athletic program. The Brothers treated sports as a self-sustaining financial affair and the primary concern was money and most of that money was cash. Admission fees to basketball and football games drove the economic engine of purchasing equipment, uniforms, and coaches' salaries.

After all the students went home after practice, Brother Maurice sat behind his desk in the Athletic Director's office educating me on the theory of coaching and its importance in the lives of our students. He found in me, a sports fan, an eager pupil and had assigned me to coach the freshman track team and suggested I build a library of books devoted to learning the intricacies of the sports. Often his discussions wandered and his conversation tilted toward a lecture on the role of sports in the general economy. Although I never witnessed him teach a class, I overheard the students talking about Brother Maurice's convoluted lectures. In the class history essay in the 1967 yearbook the editor noted that in Brother Maurice's English classes the students learned the "philosophical, sociological, geographical, historical and psychological approach to English." His Introduction to American Literature class might have been better named as Introduction to Existence.

I never missed Mass but felt less loyalty to attending Morning Prayer and during evening prayer I discovered I learned more from Brother Maurice's chitchat in the empty locker room. One exercise I rarely missed. Almost everyone attended; even Brother Maurice who would look at his watch around five o'clock and realize if we didn't hurry we'd be late.

We slept in our bedrooms on the second floor of the brothers' residence. We ate in the dining room on the first floor and lounged around in the reception room. Other than the times for prayer and Mass the chapel at one end of the first floor stood empty. The utilitarian rooms in the basement included the boiler room, the electric supply closet, the laundry room and one, almost secret room we called the recreation room, tucked in the far corner of the corridor. Its thin windows at the top of the walls near the ceiling looked out at ground level and the limited view included the undergrowth of evergreen bushes and blankets of pachysandra. While there wasn't much to see looking out, looking in wasn't easy either. The camouflage had a purpose.

Each evening at five o'clock Brother Patrick entered the recreation room and unlocked two cabinets above the wet bar. He removed a dozen bottles of liquor and lined them up on a table: several varieties of scotch, rye, vodka and gin. A small refrigerator provided ice, mixes (orange juice for screwdrivers, tomato juice for bloody marys) and garnishes: olives, maraschino cherries and bitters. The line formed quickly. We called the exercise preprandials but more informally we called it the time for drinks.

My formal education lacked any instruction in the consumption of alcohol—now I learned by doing—and I drank every day. In my family drinking occurred rarely, mostly on celebratory occasions like baptisms, confirmations and graduations. When my mother had the girls over for cards they sipped "high balls," a mixture of cheap whiskey, like Four Roses, mixed with Hoffmann ginger ale. Beer brands included Schaefer and Rheingold. At Queen of Peace I started big—scotch on the rocks which I drank slowly at first until I realized that, after forty-five minutes, Brother Patrick would return the liquor bottles to the locked closet. He'd announce the end by saying, "Last call." Brothers filled their eight and ten ounces glasses to the brim and nursed the drinks till bedtime.

We tossed the empty bottles, the dead soldiers, into a liquor box and stacked them in the boiler room. On Saturday morning Brother Patrick backed up the community station wagon to the kitchen door at the rear of the brothers' house, pulled the tailgate down and loaded the army of the dead into the cargo area. He drove to a dump and disposed of them. He reasoned that if we just threw them in the trash someone might get the wrong impression—lots of bottles had accumulated by Saturday morning. Actually, if anyone saw the dozens of bottles they would get the right impression—most of us drank too much.

Those brothers who needed more to drink found it—alcoholics displayed resourcefulness. I didn't realize the extent of the problem. One morning, during the first period of the day, as I taught my homeroom students religion, Brother Celestine waved at me from the corridor. He gestured for me to stop teaching. I excused myself from the students and stepped outside.

"You've got to help me," he said.

"Now?"

Brother Celestine stuck his head in my classroom and announced to my class that I would return in several minutes. In his stentorian voice he promised that if any student acted inappropriately he would break their arms. He hustled me down the corridor to Brother Frederick's classroom where I saw him sprawled across the floor. He must have been leaning his back against the blackboard and after he fainted he slid down the wall. Hardly conscious, he moaned when we lifted him. We dragged him out of the classroom like an injured football player being carried to the sidelines.

The brother's house is two blocks west of the school and we lugged him up the street, through the side door and up to his room. We sat him on his bed, removed his shoes, and slipped his religious habit over his head. He wore what we all wore under our habit, black pants and a white T-shirt. Brother Celestine laid him down and stayed with him while I returned to the school to inform Brother Patrick what had happened. He knew already and had taken control of Brother Frederick's religion lesson. The stunned students said nothing.

Brother Fredrick slept off the hangover and returned to teaching the next day as if nothing had happened. I don't remember any discussion, either at Queen of Peace, or any other school I taught at in the next three years, about the disease of alcoholism. Our superiors voiced more concern about those brothers who smoked cigarettes than the brothers who imbibed too much. A few mornings when I awoke with my head pounding I shirked my teaching duties by giving a surprise quiz to my classes just so the room would be quiet.

Since I earned a degree in Physics, my fate included starting graduate studies in this field. As early as February, 1965 I wrote my superiors requesting not to follow this usual procedure. I wrote presumptuously that I didn't think I'd need a graduate degree in either physics or mathematics to teach high school algebra. Instead, I suggested that I be allowed to pursue a degree in Psychology or Education. These pleas died unheeded. In

January, 1966 Brother John wrote to me about how to proceed in applying to the Department of Mathematics at Manhattan College. I procrastinated, hoping they would forget me, but in May, 1966 Brother Bernard Peter, the Director of Studies for the New York District, wrote me a blunt letter. "May we ask if you have settled on your graduate work? May I hear from you in this regard?"

Brother Alban, the Director of the Graduate Division at Manhattan College, in a letter on July 7, 1966 responded to my application with scant enthusiasm. "While your record meets the quantitative requirements set down by our graduate catalogue for the department you wish to enter, your performance in undergraduate work is found to be not qualitatively strong." Unfortunately for me, Brother Alban continued that I was to be admitted conditionally, my courses would start in the fall, and I must average a grade of B or better for my first twelve credits. Now that I wanted to abandon the scientific ship everyone threw me a life line.

I read Brother Alban's remarks as advice; select another department. In the fall of 1965 Brother Gabriel Moran arrived at Manhattan College's Department of Theology with the intention of revitalizing and expanding its mission. By the fall of 1966 the department's reputation flourished and applications to the Theology Department flooded admissions, including mine and I petitioned to withdraw from the Mathematics Department. Brother Bernard Peter sent me another pointed letter. I had been accepted by the Theology Department but he questioned the decision. Discussions by the Manhattan College faculty about my graduate studies had not been complimentary. "I just wonder," Brother Alban wrote, "how welcome you will be in the field of Theology?"

But, in a turn of events that would eventually be my salvation, Brother Augustine Loes, who had recently become the Visitor of the District, offered me an opportunity. If I accepted I would be relieved of the burden of teaching physics. The bargain appeared simple. I would be loaned to the Long Island New England (LINE) district to replace a brother who taught high school mathematics but who wished to be assigned to Lincoln Hall, a reform school as it was called, in Lincolndale, New York whose residents were already well along in their criminal careers. In order to replace him the LINE district needed a volunteer who only wanted to teach mathematics. I proved to be the ideal candidate and accepted on the condition that I would be assigned to a school in the New York City area; otherwise the deal was off. Brother Joseph, the Visitor of the LINE district wrote me a cordial welcome letter and then asked me to reconsider an appointment to Bishop Bradley High School in Manchester, New Hampshire. If I refused and cancelled the exchange I might well end up at the front of another physics class. Manchester appeared better than teaching physics. I agreed and, with an informal *quid pro quo*, asked that I be considered for a sabbatical to study theology full time after three years at Bishop Bradley. Brother Bernard Peter wrote back. "I am confident you can be placed on the Theology List for the year 1970-1971."

In the LINE district an assignment to Manchester carried the same cache as being assigned to Siberia: distant, snowy with constant temperatures below zero from late November to early March. Brothers spoke about New Hampshire as if the roads were unpaved and telephone lines had yet to be erected.

While I didn't realize the opportunity I was given, Brother Martin, the chemistry teacher at Queen of Peace did. After the June graduation as I packed my belongings one afternoon, he visited me in my room. During my two year tenure at Queen of Peace he appointed himself as my mentor, advising me about classroom decorum and reprimanding me for playing too much pinochle at night rather than preparing lessons. Don't misplay this prospect, he advised: a new school, different students, and no physics classes. At this time a debate ensued among the brothers about abandoning our religious names and using our baptismal and family names. I elected to be known as Brother Thomas and with this old new name I'd possess no history. My vocation, he continued, comprised more than just being a religious—I was called to be a teacher and if I worked at it I could be a good teacher, perhaps a great one. He dislodged me from my complacency.

The film *A Man for All Seasons* won an Oscar for best picture in 1966 and one conversation in the film, where Thomas More advised Richard Rich, impressed me greatly.

Sir Thomas More: Why not be a teacher? You'd be a fine teacher; perhaps a great one.
Richard Rich: If I was, who would know it?
Sir Thomas More: You; your pupils; your friends; God. Not a bad public, that.

I adopted this as my credo, striving to be more than good, reaching for the fine and the better, and with pluck and luck perhaps achieve greatness. Brother Martin was my Thomas More, and unlike Richard Rich, I took his advice.

The summer of 1966 posed another important decision. The time had arrived to make a decision for life. During August I attended a thirty day retreat at Barrytown, praying, meditating and contemplating one question—should I take final vows. I had no reason not to.

Until that summer I had renewed my religious vows in gradually longer time periods. After the Novitiate temporary vows lasted one year, vows were renewed in the Scholastic at first for two years and then three. During those six years I anticipated what I must finally decide. The summer of 1966 marked the end of the three year period of temporary vows. The brothers referred to the next set of vows as "final" vows but their proper name sounded more solemn. The official name of the ceremony was "perpetual religious profession."

In the summer of 1968 at Barrytown I engaged mostly in spiritual reading but started studying old letters. My five years in the Scholasticate had allowed me to enroll in courses a bit far afield of my requirements. During the fall semester of 1964 I muddled along with Cs and Ds in physics but earned a grade of A in a religious education course entitled "Preparing for Christian Marriage." I decided to take this class for one reason, the professor, Father Gerard Sloyan, a noted expert in the field of the Christian liturgy would teach the course. I felt uncomfortable in my religious habit surrounded mostly by females and counter to my usual custom I sat in the back of the room.

During the semester I met a female student. We got acquainted and started speaking to each other outside of class. As the semester progressed, I felt my attitude toward her evolve into a friendship; Platonic, at first. She confided in me that she had boyfriends and that revelation put the brakes on wherever it was my mind was racing. At the end of the semester my main worry concerned comprehensive exams and when the semester ended our friendship might have ended except we wrote to each other for the next year.

She remained in Washington while I went to Queen of Peace. The letters lengthened and I finally shelved Platonic into my subconscious and withdrew romantic. My carefully constructed letters would provide the spontaneous combustion for our relationship. As the end of the thirty day retreated approached I needed to make a decision. I wrote a long letter leading to my willingness to forgo final vows for her. She wrote back that she couldn't accept this proposition because she didn't want to be the reason I lost my vocation. If she considered my proposal presumptuous, bordering on brazen, but certainly ill-conceived she never said so. What was I thinking? We'd never dated.

I never held her hand and I certainly hadn't kissed her except for a sisterly peck on the cheek.

On Sunday, August 28, 1966 I, now Brother Thomas Brennan and no longer Brother Peter Terrence, accompanied by thirty other brothers, promised and vowed "poverty, chastity, obedience, stability in the said Society [Brothers of the Christian Schools] and to teach the poor gratuitously…inviolably all my lifetime."

Once again the mantra "Not to decide is to decide" the proverb widely attributed to Harvey Cox, a theologian at the Harvard Divinity School weaved through my mind. That's what I did on that August Sunday. I didn't decide to remain a brother; I decided not to leave the order.

A week later I arrived at Bishop Bradley High School in a city many had convinced me was the outpost of civilization, Manchester, New Hampshire.

Chapter 20

If I retraced my career to erect a historical marker for the turning point in my life as a teacher it would be the front door of Bishop Bradley High School. As Brother Thomas, rather than Brother Peter, I started my teaching career anew. Buoyed by Brother Martin's counsel and motivated by a fresh urge to teach well, I dedicated two hours of preparation for every hour of instruction. Some nights I prepared my classes well past midnight. Never once in my two years in Manchester did I play pinochle.

Although my title read "mathematics chairman" and one its few perks included choosing what courses I would teach, Brother Owen, the assistant principal, had already determined my teaching schedule for the fall of 1967. I taught religion to my freshman homeroom class, introductory algebra, an intermediate algebra/trigonometry and a pre-calculus course to bright juniors. The pre-calculus course lacked a textbook and I choose one by Mary Dolciani, one of the better textbooks of the time. By December I had solved every problem in the text and I had prepared enough material to teach well into July and August. The students responded enthusiastically by insisting that next year I teach a section of introductory calculus. This I refused to do admitting it was beyond my grasp.

The religious community at Bishop Bradley fared little better than the one at Queen of Peace. Several brothers on the faculty tried to invigorate our liturgy. Brother Anthony the First (there were two Brothers Anthony) selected more appropriate readings for our liturgies and Brother John, who could sing reasonably, led us in meaningful hymns. Brother Anthony, a vivacious Italian whose laugh lasted nearly a half a minute, peppered his religion classes, in a style similar to Brother Maurice at Queen of Peace, with allusions to Buddha and critiques of Confucius. Every school had a renaissance man as a teacher.

The fall semester of 1967 moved rapidly but in the spring of 1968 even remote Manchester felt the earthquake of American politics as it rattled institutions including the Catholic Church. The Brothers tended to ignore the academic discipline of political theory. In my five years at Catholic University I never enrolled in a course in political science. At Queen of Peace I rarely read newspapers except for the sports scores.

At Bishop Bradley I met political junkies. The community subscribed to *The New York Times* and every morning two copies lay on the table in the common room. I read *Time*, *Newsweek*, *Commonweal* and *America* from cover to cover. In early February 1968 every newspaper and magazine published and republished the famous Vietnam War photo snapped by Eddie Adams. Two men stood on a Saigon street. Police Chief Nguyen Ngoc Loan's back was to the camera while his Vietcong prisoner, Nguyn Van Lem faced the photographer. One could argue this picture of Loan's execution of Lem started the end of the Vietnam War. Less than a month later Walter Cronkite concluded his nightly news broadcast with a personal reflection on the stage of the war—it wasn't going well.

Immediately the topic of war invaded our history and religion classes. Like most segments of society at that time our religious community was divided along age lines—the young brothers spoke out against the war, the older ones argued patriotism. Each side remained entrenched but the arguments continued.

There was only one television in the community. I didn't watch it much, except for the news, but some Brothers watched any show broadcast. In January 1968 NBC launched a new comedy series, *Laugh-In*, that, among other skits, lampooned politics. Rather than argue with the television regulars, a half-dozen of us trotted over to the school and watched Rowan and Martin religiously from 8 to 8:30 each Monday night and often hung around the darkened school discussing politics, religion, sex, the religious life and any topic *Laugh-In's* troupe threw at us.

After Martin Luther King's murder on April 4 in Memphis the silliness ended but isolated Manchester, New Hampshire, with a miniscule minority population, avoided the riots exploding around the country. While my spiritual reading remained minimal, a friend of Thomas Merton, Daniel Berrigan, a Jesuit priest, burst onto the political stage. In May 1968 Berrigan and several other peace activists (they didn't like the negative term war protestors) broke into the Selective Service office in Catonsville, Maryland and with homemade napalm burned hundred of draft files.

Many conservative Catholics marginalized Berrigan and the Catonsville 9 as kooks at best and traitors at worst. Although Berrigan acted as an individual, his priestly garb stood out. What might have happened if, next to Berrigan, a bishop or cardinal had stood hand in hand? Would the government have tried Cardinal Cushing and sentenced him to do time in the federal penitentiary in Danbury, Connecticut?

I subscribed to their arguments against the war and began reading Merton again. His book *Conjectures of a Guilty Bystander*, published in 1965, revealed a Merton I, and most Catholics, didn't recognize. In the introduction Merton writes that "I do not have clear answers to current questions. I do have questions, and, as a matter of fact, I think a man is known better by his questions than by his answers."[18] I started at home and began asking questions about myself.

While I and the other younger brothers moved to the political left, the contemporary political reality of Manchester, already political right, moved even further in that direction. New Hampshire politicians espoused a Republican agenda spurred by William Loeb, the publisher and editor of the *Manchester Union Leader*, the only paper in the city. Loeb was a conservative's conservative and apologized to no one for his positions. He defended the actions of Senator Joseph McCarthy so pigeon-holing his political positions proved easy.

Bishop Bradley High School drained many of the academically talented students from the Manchester public schools. While the school didn't make the front pages of his paper, critical comments about the school often appeared in letters to the editor where fact and fiction blended into illusive half truths. The Brothers concluded Loeb harbored not only anti-catholic feelings in general but specifically toward Bishop Bradley High School as an institution that misrepresented Catholic dogma. Finally, Loeb flew the first public punch and the school landed face down with a critical editorial on the front page.

Brother John used literature in his religion classes to make relevant points about theological issues. One religious topic in the late 1960s concerned what it meant to be real as opposed to being disingenuous; what it meant to be a real person and hence a real Christian. The premise, love can make you real, neatly summarized the issue.

One day Brother John asked his students to explore this question by having them respond to a quotation from "I Love You," a poster designed by Corita Kent, at the time, a sister in the order of the Immaculate Heart of Mary. One of her best known works, a 150 foot rainbow, stretched across a Boston Gas (now Keyspan) tank on the Southeast expressway. She created a similar design for the 1985 stamp "Love."

The poster contained a passage selected from *The Velveteen Rabbit*, Margery Williams's classic children's book published in 1922 and still in print when it and the poster became the focus of a brouhaha in Manchester. I don't believe the poster identified the source of the passage.

In the beginning of the novella, the Velveteen Rabbit and another character named the Skin Horse engaged in a conversation about reality. In one passage the narrator describes The Skin Horse as being "so old that his brown coat was bald in patches and showed the seams underneath, and most of the hairs in his tail and most of the hairs in his tail had been pulled out." The velveteen rabbit asks the Skin Horse how a toy becomes real. "Does it mean having things that buzz inside you and a stick out handle?"

In a front-page lead editorial, disguised as an article, the writer analyzed these, and other similar passages, concluding the entire book represented a shady allegory of pornography. The Skin Horse was a penis running amok through a child's play room. He claimed the story hid its author's true purpose and the brothers' collaboration in immorality—to proselytize students into becoming sex addicts.

Letters to the editor flew furiously. Loeb attempted to use them in subsequent editorials the same way he used the story and compounded the issue by implying the Brothers' community consisted of a horde of homosexuals.

Brother Anthony learned the source of the passage and went "book in hand [and] showed him the passage." Some days later Loeb and the *Union Leader* tried to weasel from their predicament in a retraction editorial entitled "A Sticky Wicket," an editorial filled with double speak and gobbledygook.

The Velveteen Rabbit incident would be our tempest in a teapot. Far more tragic events arrived in the early summer. When I awoke on Wednesday morning June 5, my thoughts turned to the last two weeks of school and how I needed to push my students to finish the year well. As I shaved and dressed, the news announcer on the radio confirmed Robert Kennedy's death in a hotel kitchen in California.

Everything began to change.

ℬ℞

During my two tenure of teaching mathematics at Bishop Bradley I learned from both the good teachers and the bad ones. Brother Owen, the Vice-Principal, taught one section of mathematics and I often conferred with him on how the curriculum might be improved. New Hampshire, like New Jersey lacked state-wide examinations, so we decided the curriculum according to our own wishes.

The bad mathematics teacher, an independently wealthy man, taught for the paltry sum of one dollar a year and replacing him with a salaried teacher threatened the financial stability of the school. Bishop Bradley, like most Catholic high schools, was a tuition driven institution with no luxuries like an endowment. When I arrived the man had been teaching for more than twenty years. Brother Owen, to minimize his influence, relegated him to teaching two courses: Geometry to sophomores and business mathematics to seniors. While sophomores could be intimidated to behave, seniors were less pliable. While he droned about the nuances of mortgage calculations in the front of the classroom, the seniors tried to stay awake in the back. His cardinal sins of teaching included a monotone delivery with his back toward the students and his blackboard notes resembled the Cyrillic alphabet.

Infrequently, I politely suggested he consider other methods of teaching but after so many years of doing it one way he found it impossible to change. He had graduated from Harvard with both a bachelor's degree and a master's in Business Administration but intelligence ranks as a minor virtue of a good teacher. With three graduate degrees I listened to many intelligent persons stand in front of a classroom who rambled incoherently and believed they were teaching.

One of the reasons I think I was a good teacher is that I had so much experience being a poor student; I understood the futility of trying to comprehend. I doubted I would ever learn the arcana of Latin and Mathematics and what I did learn came slowly. When my students failed to grasp an idea their faces crinkled and their heads shook as if warding off a swarm of bees. Stanislavski remarked about acting, but I applied it to teaching, that "average people have no conception of how to observe the facial expression, the look of the eye, the tone of the voice, in order to comprehend the state of mind of the persons [students] with whom they talk."[19]

Despite my suggestions to this teacher, I, and most likely anyone else, could not help him be a good teacher. Stanislavski continued; "You cannot put into a person what he does not possess."[20]

I suggested to Brother Owen that for the next school year he should assign me to teach senior math. Many of the juniors I taught in intermediate algebra and trigonometry showed promise and I devised a course I called "Analysis," a combination of pre-calculus, set theory and mathematical induction. I dared to inject a brief discussion of the limits of functions, one of the first topics in calculus, and saw on the faces of some students the same incomprehension I had felt when I failed Calculus I in my first year of the Scholasticate in Troy.

One of the sisters at Immaculata High School, a girl's school about two blocks away from Bishop Bradley, encountered the same problem with her seniors. We arranged to team teach the Analysis course. I would teach the odd chapters and she would teach the even chapters. One benefit to both of us included half as much lesson preparation. During the first week of school I taught a chapter at Bishop Bradley and the following week I taught the same chapter at Immaculata, my first experience teaching girls. They acted more docile than boys, their neater written exams proved easier to correct, and I found them attractive when they giggled innocently. The brothers' schools employed only male teachers and the schools the nuns administered employed only female teachers. As I walked into the classroom at Immaculata, I felt as lost as a lifeboat in the ocean; a male bobbing in a sea of teenage females. Since I usually called my students by their first names, I continued the practice but addressing Jane, Eileen, Wendy and the dozen others sounded too intimate to me. The novelty of a male teacher, however, soon wore thin. The girls, unaccustomed to initiating discussions, refrained from asking questions so I peppered them with questions, assigned heavy loads of homework and created challenging exams. They thrived, and in the field of mathematics historically dominated by males, I thought my class of girls might make some dent in the gender gap among mathematicians. Several of them were exceptionally bright.

One afternoon, during that first week of school in September 1968, Brother Adrian Talbot the principal, asked me to meet him in his office. His furtive invitation, lacking any hint of why he wanted to speak with me, sent my mind into conspiracy mode. Had I been improper teaching the girls? Was calling them by their first names too forthcoming? Or had I committed an even greater transgression?

I sat down. He shut the door—not a good sign for me—in the brothers' schools the principal's door rarely closed. We always referred to Brother Adrian as Tal—short for his surname Talbot—and he hemmed for a moment before blurting out his predicament. I figured I was the problem but I wasn't. Tal asked if I had noticed one of the physical education teachers had not yet reported to his classes. I said I hadn't. He advised me to keep the information on the hush-hush; the man would not be returning to Bishop Bradley. Brother Owen arranged for the students in his classes to be redistributed to other gym teachers and Brother Owen explained to the students that the gym teacher's family in Rhode Island needed him for some unstated indefinite emergency. I sighed with relief that Tal's problem excluded me but I wondered what role I would play in this problem. It looked like a solution had already been found.

Tal continued and disclosed the underlying predicament. Besides the man's position as a gym teacher he also served as the Athletic Director for the school. One of his responsibilities involved collecting the admission monies at football and basketball games and depositing them in a separate bank account used for athletic expenses. Evidently lots of twenty and fifty dollars bills collected in New Hampshire now circulated in Rhode Island—the man was a thief—and how would I like to be Athletic Director. My actual title was Assistant Athletic Director to continue the ruse that the teacher might be returning. Brother Maurice's lectures at Queen of Peace about the role of an athletic director would come in handy.

The next Saturday afternoon I lingered around the admission gate to the first home football game and watched one dollar bills turn into tens and tens into fifties. At half-time, I packed all the money into a suitcase and stuck the suitcase into the trunk of a police car. I hopped into the passenger seat and the policeman escorted me back to the school where I put the suitcase in the far corner of the athletic director's office.

On Sunday morning I counted the money and wrote a report for Tal. He compared my report with the reports of the previous year and the extent of the theft exceeded his own estimates.

Saturday high school football games in New Hampshire garnered capacity crowds and halfway through the season the athletic bank account contained enough money to buy new uniforms for every team in the school. I made the salesman from Champion Sportswear a happy man.

As Athletic Director I assumed another minor responsibility—the moderator of the cheerleaders. I knew some of these girls since I taught them in the Analysis math class. I monitored their practices in the gym and, while my relationship with them remained teacher and student some of them started confiding in me as a counselor. One girl confessed she couldn't wait until the day after graduation when she would enlist with the Army to escape her father. What about college I asked. You're smart, I insisted, an A student, even in difficult courses like my Analysis class. My father, she said, doesn't even think I should be in high school. As a 60s liberal I felt sad that joining the military solved her problem.

Chapter 21

During my two years at Bishop Bradley High School I lived on two planes of life. The first involved my teaching life as I tried to hone my skills. I prepared each lesson carefully devoting the beginning of each class to questions from students, followed by a presentation of material with enough examples to last the entire class and at the end an assignment geared to reinforce what I had just taught.

In the construction of my quizzes and tests I attempted to learn what my students knew, not what they didn't know, and I marked each test carefully, praising those who performed well and encouraging those who didn't

On October 15, 1967 I entered the high school book store and requested some stationary supplies for my classes: chalk, erasers, notebooks, pens and pencils. I brought most of these materials to my homeroom class, stored them in the supply closet but brought one thick notebook back to my room in the Brothers' house. That night I started writing about the other segment of my life: my psychological state, my spiritual life, my interior doubts and the writing assumed the semblance of having a conversation with myself. I continued entries in this journal until January 31, 1971 more than three years after I started. I wrote two more entries in the journal after then but that was the important date.

Among the many entries there were few facts. I hardly noted the weather although I mentioned the first snowfall occurred on November 16. Living in New England in the winter should have triggered much rumination about cold, snow and ice but my writing ignored the ten-foot snow piles in the school parking lot. The natives of New England accepted falling snow like Floridians accepted growing grass. It happened—and happened often. In my two years at Bishop Bradley, Brother Adrian, the principal, cancelled classes only once and not because of any northeaster. That morning at breakfast he announced he called off classes because the batteries on the school buses had frozen—the 6 A.M. temperature topped out at -23° Fahrenheit. Later that morning when the temperature warmed up to the negative low teens, I walked across the parking lot to do some class work. I breathed normally and felt my lungs tingle like pins and needles. Holding my breath so my lungs didn't hurt, I hurried into the school building.

Much of the journal writing reflected my attempt at non-rhyming, free verse poetry with scant idea of either meter or enjambment. Writing poetry only involved expressing my feelings and the primary emotion was loneliness.

The first entry that October evening was entitled "Alone." A case could be made that my mental state approached clinical depression but in fact my feelings of lonesomeness comprised adolescent emotions I should have felt ten years earlier in my life. The last line of the poem suggested my emotional developed lagged by ten years. "I must die now; I can not bear to live." Quite melodramatic and hardly literal; I never contemplated suicide and felt quite sad when I heard of someone who succeeded.

Beside poetry I composed essays on psychological and theological topics: energy, the nature of a religious community, prayer, the future of religions and in my writing I attempted to find answers to questions I had not yet fully formulated.

I went to the movies quite often and often alone. One of my students worked as the ticket usher in the lone theater in downtown Manchester. He informed me of the upcoming films and on slow nights he whisked me in without a ticket. He resembled the kid in the old Philip Morris cigarette ad with his red jacket, chevrons and gold buttons. I might have been tempted to inflate his grades as a favor but his grades couldn't go much higher.

Much of my reading included explanations of cinematography and how to evaluate a good film from a bad one. I read *The Cinema as Art* by Ralph Stephenson and learned the techniques of film and Pauline Kael and Judith Crist for their reviews.

Watching films stimulated my self-examination. I started asking questions about myself. Yes, I had a vocation but why did I have it? Yes, I felt quite alone but was it possible to become friends with someone and yet still keep my vocation. Films mattered to me and I tried to analyze how they affected me or what I could learn from them. Was I as insane as Alan Bates in *King of Hearts*, one of the many anti-war films of that era? Had I been bamboozled like Mountain Rivera in *Requiem for a Heavyweight*?

At about this time the filmmaker Ingmar Bergmann asked similar questions in his films; was God silent? Can death be postponed? I believed in God but He felt more remote as if either He or I were withdrawing from each other like spouses in bad marriage. During Christmas and spring vacations I stopped searching for God; instead I sought out the art movie houses of Greenwich Village in New York City where they showed Bergman films constantly. Maybe Bergman had some answers to my theological questions. He titled some films with obvious scriptural references: *The Seventh Seal*, an apocalyptic reference from Revelations and *Through a Glass Darkly* echoed the next to last verse in St. Paul's famous explanation in 1 Corinthians 13 of why charity is the greatest of all virtues; "We see now through a glass, darkly, but then face to face." I often wondered if Bergman consciously filmed the famous scene in *Persona*, where the profiles of Liv Ullmann and Bibi Andersson merge into one face.

On weekends, some of the brother of the brothers travelled to Boston to see films that weren't popular enough to make the cinema in Manchester. While returning from one of these films I dominated the conversation in the station wagon with my analysis of the film. Brother Anthony yelled at me, "Stop. Why are you picking the film apart?" I had an answer—I had too many questions about my own life. He said, "Can't you just watch a film and enjoy it?" I admitted I couldn't do that.

Besides films I read novels that promoted reflection. After reading Nikos Kazantzakis's *Zorba the Greek* I wrote that I should learn to dance. And I started discussing my feeling with girls, older sisters of my Immaculata students and their friends. At the end of my second year at Bradley I had a conversation with a girl named Carolyn. I had gotten to know her well enough to be invited by her family to dinner one Sunday evening in June 1968. Her parents served a typical New England summer meal: corn, potato salad, coleslaw and, in my honor since I was leaving Bishop Bradley, boiled lobster. I sat in my chair and stared at the dead, red crustacean dripping water colored by sage green tomalley.

Someone noticed my ignorance and said, "You've never eaten lobster before, have you?"

I said, "No. I haven't." That provided a little laugh for everyone—what did New Yorkers eat on special occasions—and they advised me how to use the cracker and the tiny picks to get at all the lobster meat. I displayed my naiveté in many matters.

The next morning when I thanked Carolyn for the invitation she casually informed me that I would soon be withdrawing from the religious life. I told her I didn't think so but wondered if my decorum or conversation at the dinner revealed more about my inner struggles than I would have wanted.

During these two years I thought I confronted these issues alone but I didn't. I wish I had known so many others suffered the same uncertainties as I did. When a brother withdrew from the order no one announced it; the fact circulated slowly. In the six years from the beginning of the Novitiate in July of 1959 until my group's graduation from Catholic University in June of 1964 only eight brothers in that Novitiate group withdrew, four of them in the Novitiate year alone which was certainly understandable. Some people quickly evaluated that the religious life was not for them. Six more withdrew during my two years at Queen of Peace and just as I embarked on my journey to Manchester in the summer of 1967, six more withdrew. I never saw it coming.

A similar pattern of withdrawal from the brothers occurred with other Novitiate classes. With fewer brothers available schools closed: St. Augustine's in Brooklyn in 1969, Manhattan College Preparatory School in 1972 and the list grew each year. What should have been an unmistakable sign to me that, as Bob Dylan's lyrics goes, "the times were a-changin" was the closure of the Juniorate in 1968 followed the next year by the closing of the Novitiate. On the battlefield of the religious life there were no troops behind us.

A small vignette about the Novitiate community just prior to its closing clarified how the religious community of novices and their worship had changed. In an article in the March/April 1967 edition of *The Catholic Worker*

Dorothy Day wrote in her "On Pilgrimage" column about her encounter with the brothers at Barrytown. She had established a farm in nearby Tivoli to supply vegetables to the soup kitchens of New York City.

"When we moved up the Hudson we had never lived near the Christian Brothers and knew little of them...[they] knew that we wanted to get a garden in, a big one to feed our multitude and some of the multitude of the Bowery. So one of the Brothers came over and ploughed up a field for us, giving us a good start in preparing the land, which had been used as pasture for many years...Every Saturday at eleven-fifteen we go to the Mass sung by the Brothers and some of the students, a folk Mass accompanied by four guitars. The music is haunting and the words descriptive of what the Mass is. Afterwards, we are always invited to lunch—even when we bring a dozen people."[21] Worship had changed; with the liturgy now celebrated in English, the hootenanny influenced the music and Gregorian chant disappeared.

After remaining vacant for five years the brothers sold the Barrytown property to Rev. Moon's Unification Church in 1974. An era in the history of the Brothers of the Christian Schools ended.

This pattern of withdrawal from the religious life invaded not just the Brothers of the Christian Schools but other male religious orders: the Marist Brothers (they closed their Juniorate in Esopus, New York in 1969), the Xaverian Brothers and the Congregation of the Christian Brothers, an order often confused with ours, also experienced massive withdrawals. We called the latter group the Irish Christian Brothers since they were founded in Ireland by Edmund Rice.

Even more remarkable numbers of withdrawal occurred within the women's religious orders. Here the statistics staggered the imagination of what upheaval occurred in the Catholic Church. According to Helen Rose Fuchs Ebaugh's study *Out of the Cloister* the number of American female religious in 1964 topped 180,000. Twelve years later that number was 131,000 a reduction of 49,000 sisters.[22]

Some commentators on these times attribute the dissolution of the religious orders and the more general upheaval in the Catholic Church to Vatican II. The council, rather than the cause, was more likely a catalyst. It would have happened anyway.

The exodus continued. According to the Center for Applied Research in the Apostolate at Georgetown University the number of female religious in the United States in 2008 was 59,000. Some estimates report an average age of sixty-five. Some orders will become extinct.

In November 1968, while I wrote my own questions and searched for answers, William Ammentorp completed his exhaustive study of the order, *The Committed: A Sociological Study of the Brothers of the Christian Schools.*[23] Each community of brothers in the United States received a copy. On the inside cover of mine, Brother Adrian wrote, in a handwriting I can still indentify, "Bishop Bradley Comm." It sat, unread, on a bookshelf in the common room; finally I stole it and read it like it was a forbidden book, pouring through it trying to find myself in the composite portraits of different kinds of brothers: the active brother, the recluse, the rebel; who was I? In the chapter entitled "Crisis in the Religious Life," Ammentorp asked several pointed questions. To the statement "Brothers benefit by associating with women" 70% answered "strongly agree" or "agree" while only 6% "disagreed" and 1% "strongly disagreed." [24] I know I agreed and the stage was set; I stood alone and wondered what characters would enter my life. In the conclusion to the study Ammentorp remarked that "it should be clear from the [study] that the committed life is still a viable possibility." True, but for whom? Many are called; few are chosen.

Chapter 22

When I arrived at Manhattan College in June 1969 I experienced a religious environment that differed from my previous communities in unexpected ways.

I lived with twelve brothers at Queen of Peace for two years and almost twenty brothers at Bishop Bradley the next two years. In the Manhattan College community more than thirty brothers resided at the West Hill estate on Fieldston Road in the exclusive Riverdale section of the Bronx. All the private streets, patrolled by a security police force that enforced the prohibition of public parking, created the impression of a well-maintained ghost town.

The bucolic grounds, about a half mile north of the main Manhattan College campus, resembled much of the surrounding Riverdale estates: tall chestnut trees and twelve foot rhododendrons dominated the property. To accommodate the increase of residential students, Manhattan College brought the property in the early 1960s.   Several buildings dotted the property: small cottages, a barracks-like building and a two storey mansion where the college prefects lived during the school year.   When I moved in I heard tales about the property's former name, West Hill Hospital, a residential psychiatric facility where, rumor had it, that one of the more frequent treatments included electroshock therapy. Despite my curiosity I never found evidence of its former use except for one strange architectural feature; in St. Joseph's Hall, the large, mostly barren recreation room, lightly furnished with several lounge chairs, a table and a TV, the entire floor was solid concrete.

Since I lived in the last room at the end of the corridor on the second floor of St. Joseph's Hall, I had the luxury of two catty-corner windows and with the help of a small fan created a cross breeze at night to counter the heat.

Not only did the brothers come from the New York District but others arrived from Baltimore, Chicago, St. Louis and San Francisco. I discovered they enjoyed an interest in sports and conversation with the brothers from the Baltimore schools proved easy. Throughout the summer we followed the fortunes of the New York Mets and the Baltimore Orioles who met in the World Series that October. On many evenings we lounged in the chairs on the concrete floor of the recreation room and argued the merits of Tom Seaver, the phenomenal   Mets   pitcher,   versus   Brooks Robinson, the all-star third baseman for the Orioles. Good pitching will beat good hitting, I argued, and to my, and most of the New York fan's surprise, the Miracle Mets, as they came to be known, won their first World Series that October in five games after losing the first one. The brothers from Baltimore sat befuddled in the front of the TV—the Mets?

But another community resided at Manhattan that summer. Next to St. Joseph's Hall stood a small cottage that housed a dozen other religious—nuns—women—and the sisters and brothers at West Hill evolved into a hybrid religious community. We celebrated mass together each morning at the mansion in an ornate sunroom converted into a chapel, grabbed a quick breakfast in the dining room and then walked together through the rustic streets of Riverdale to our courses on the main campus.

. We sat next to each other in classes, ate lunch together and often met in study groups in the evening. The nuns dressed in modified habits, skirts ending at the knee rather than the ankles, and short veils replacing traditional wimples. Some wore a cross hanging from their neck or a religious pin in their blouse label.

These nuns, cut from a different religious cloth then those who taught me at St. John's, belonged to religious teaching orders similar to the Christian Brothers: the Sisters of Charity of New York, the Dominicans and the Religious of the Sacred Heart of Mary. All of these nuns held undergraduate degrees and, like the brothers, had majored in English, History and Mathematics before they entered the classroom. They taught in colleges and high schools and in their schools implemented the directives of the Council of Vatican II with equal vigor as they attempted to revitalize the liturgy of the Catholic Church. We shared a common purpose.

As June turned into July, we anticipated the date of Sunday July 20 when Apollo 11 would land of the surface of the moon. An ad hoc committee organized a liturgy for the following Monday evening that would coincide with Neil Armstrong's moon walk and we dubbed the event the "moon mass."

That evening we gathered in one of the college houses on campus where one of the professors, Donald Gray, had an office. About eight o' clock several dozen of us crowded around a portable black and white TV, adjusted its rabbit ears, and watched the news accounts leading up to the time of the first moon walk.

To my surprise, the CBS announcer, Walter Cronkite, confirmed a rumor that one of the astronauts, Buzz Aldrin, had brought two unusual items to the moon: a vial of wine and a small communion bread loaf consecrated by his Presbyterian pastor. Buzz made a short statement about how this moment would be an appropriate moment to meditate and administered to himself the first communion on the moon.

Just before eleven our small group of sisters and brothers watched with 600 million other people on earth as Neil Armstrong stepped into the dust of the Sea of Tranquility. We turned the TV volume down and the Canadian priest from Nova Scotia, Father John MacDonald who studied with us, celebrated the liturgy. As was the custom of the time, guitars replaced organs and folk songs replaced Gregorian chant. For a brief moment, not only was all right with the world, but with the universe.

Brother Gabriel Moran, the director of the theology program, developed a rigorous curriculum around the central issues of Vatican II. The required readings included several prominent theologians of the time: Hans Kung, Eduord Schillebeeckx, John McQuarrie, Harvey Cox and himself. Herder and Herder, a prominent theological publishing house, had marketed Brother Gabriel's doctoral dissertation at the Catholic University of America with the title *Revelation* and in the next decade Brother Gabriel wrote several more books linking theology and catechetics.

While many students had only heard of Brother's Gabriel's enthusiastic teaching, I had experienced it in the Scholasticate where he taught several courses in Religion and Philosophy. Only rare teachers can make Hume, Locke and Rousseau interesting and Brother Gabriel taught them enthusiastically. Rumors circulated that he had a photographic memory and he delivered his lectures with only the assistance of a half-dozen index cards. During one class in the Scholasticate I thought he had wandered a bit in his presentation. Speaking about John Dewey, he explained how the man and his philosophy of education had been widely misunderstood. "Here's Dewey's own words, "he said. Then he said, "Quote" and cited a passage from one of Dewey's books. He continued speaking for several minutes and I started to think about what were Dewey's words and what was Brother Gabriel's explanation. After several more minutes

Brother Gabriel said, "Unquote." This was no joke—he had quoted Dewey verbatim. The disbelievers easily verified the source since Brother Gabriel cited the chapter and page numbers. Many years later at lunch I reminded him of this incident. He admitted he had a photographic memory.

While Brother's Gabriel explained the more arcane aspects of philosophy he also concentrated on how our use of language frames an issue. He emphasized that little words, like "in" and "that" change the meaning of fundamental words like "faith" and "believe." In his lectures he made distinctions between the phrases "belief in" and "belief that" and argued they were not synonymous. When he was elected the head of the Long Island New England district in 19xx he called himself the *president* of the district rather than the *provincial*.

I had spent the summers of 1967 and 1968 taking theology courses at Manhattan and had already earned twelve credits toward my master's degree. In the summer of 1969 I took two courses: Salvation Theology of the Old Testament taught by Brother Gabriel and The Theology of St. Paul (Theology 765). Most of the day I spent in classes and, in the evening went to the library and read the textbooks from cover to cover late into the night.

I started discussing ideas more thoroughly with one nun, Sister Ann Porter, a member of the Religious of the Sacred Heart of Mary. We differed in many ways. In class I sat in the front and asked many questions; she sat in the back and listened. I spoke loudly, she softly. At six feet two inches I was a foot taller. Growing up in the

Bronx I rooted for the New York Yankees; she grew up in Everett, Massachusetts, a working-class suburb north of Boston where her father took her to Fenway Park and she cheered for my arch enemy, the Red Sox. I majored in Physics and taught mathematics; she majored in the Classics and taught Horace and Virgil. The two of us definitively proved that opposites attract like magnets. I was a north pole, she was a south and we bonded.

During the fall semester Brother Patrick McGary, a history professor at Manhattan College, invited me to preview a film not yet released. I knew Brother Patrick from the Novitiate and the Scholasticate. He entered the Novitiate at an older age than most vocations and the usual explanation, in cases like his, centered on the theory of a "delayed vocation." His interest in movies as an art form was as serious as mine and one afternoon I accompanied him to a showing at the Columbia Pictures studio on Fifth Avenue.

The film producers arranged previews for several organizations. Brother Patrick introduced me to the Director of the Catholic Legion of Decency, an organization dedicated to countering the influence of immoral films. When I grew up the Legion of Decency wielded enormous power over the commercial success or failure of a film.

Its initial evaluation system, maintained until the late 1960s, made it easy to comprehend: an "A" rating indicated a film as "morally unobjectionable," "B" stood for "morally unobjectionable in part" and "C" meant "condemned." Monsignor Scanlan posted the monthly list on the bulletin board in the vestibule of St. John's Church. I usually scanned the list from the bottom up.

During the 1950s several popular films earned a "C" classification, mainly for their salaciousness and lack of sexual mores: *And God Created Woman* which launched the American career of Bridgette Bardot in 1954 and in the same year *Baby Doll*, the first film to be approved by the Motion Picture Production Code by condemned by the Legion of Decency. If the Legion of Decency labeled a film with a rating of C for condemned as immoral the film stood little chance of becoming a commercially viable but by 1969 the Legion of Decency, now renamed the National Catholic Office for Motion Pictures exerted less influence on the movie habits of American Catholics especially since it condemned *The Pawnbroker* in 1964 which examined the consequences of Jews who survived the concentration camps and Rosemary's Baby in 1968 which raised theological questions albeit from Satan's point of view. From the summer of 1969 to the summer of 1970 I reviewed several hundred films; some so dreadful they were never released to the public.

In the early spring of 1970 Brother Patrick told me about a film I missed previewing, *Butch Cassidy and the Sundance Kid* starring Paul Newman and Robert Redford. It had been released in the fall of 1969 but Twentieth Century Fox studios re-released it in the spring of 1970 since it had been nominated for seven Academy Awards. On the surface the movie appeared to conform to the stereotypical western with a dash of romance, but it contained several distinguishing features: an off-tune melody by Bert Bacharach (Raindrop Keep Falling on my Head), sepia toning of still photographs that created a bygone era, and Paul Neuman of *Hud* and *Cool Hand Luke* fame now cast as a bon vivant bank robber. *Butch Cassidy*, Sister Ann and I came together one spring Saturday evening.

I didn't think it would be quite so easy. Casually, I mentioned to her that I planned to see the film and would she like to accompany me. She accepted immediately and we arranged to meet on the main campus to maintain some anonymity; if particular friendships with male religious was dangerous, particular friendships with female religious was nuclear. We walked up Waldo Avenue to the theater on Riverdale Avenue. One romantic scene in the film involves Paul Newman clowning around as he rides a bike. After the film we walked back down Waldo Avenue but instead of heading back to West Hill we detoured down to Broadway. Sister Ann told me she couldn't ride a bike which I found quite unbelievable. I related my childhood accidents riding down Summit Place making them a bit more adventurous than they were at the time. With my expertise, I assured her, I could teach her in five minutes. As we walked and discussed the film our swaying hands hit each other. Rather than let go we held hands. My breathing quickened, my heart pressed against my chest, I lost a pound, all in sweat, and have never shook so violently in my life. We didn't say much, thankfully; I would have sounded like a baby babbling. We continued along Broadway, turned up 254th Street to West Hill on Fieldston Road and said good night. Maybe, I suggested, we'd see another movie next Saturday night.

Chapter 23

Now what? I had a vocation and had pronounced final vows—an oath—words to God that I would dedicate my life to teaching as a Brother of the Christian Schools. I was also in love. One precluded the other.

In the late 1970s some novel theories circulated about how the religious life might be lived in the future. One idea bandied around imagined both men and women living together in a religious community. A variation on this concept maintained religious might even get married, since chastity, the second vow religious professed, did not per se include celibacy. Most agreed any arrangement of this kind would be squashed by the Catholic Church whose history of sex and spirituality meant keeping them mutually exclusive.

A second theory maintained that most brothers possessed only a temporary vocation, a life of limited time within the order. When that temporary period expired a brother would be free to withdraw from the order. A cursory examination of the statistics indicated this constituted more than a theory—it was the reality of all religious orders from 1960 to 1980.

A staggering number of withdrawals occurred within the women's religious orders. The statistics only hint at the upheaval occurring in the Catholic Church. According to Helen Rose Fuchs Ebaugh's studies, *Women in the Vanishing Cloister* and *Out of the Cloister*, the number of American female religious rose to 168,527 religious sisters in the United States in 1960.[25] Four years later the number had climbed 7.5% to 181,421.[26] Twelve years later that number was 131,000 a reduction of 49,000. The dire situation excluded far worse numbers; many religious withdrew from their orders without any processing, AWOL, and some, the most jaded, left the Catholic Church entirely. Roman Catholics comprise the largest religious affiliation in the United States while Baptists are numbered second. A joke among Catholics is that the Baptists are really third—lapsed Catholics are second.

The exodus continued. According to the Center for Applied Research in the Apostolate at Georgetown University, the number of female religious in the United States in 2008 was 59,000. Some estimates report the average age of these women at greater than sixty-five years. Some orders will become extinct.

On a smaller scale, I professed final vows with thirty other brothers in the summer of 1967. Of that number, twenty-six withdrew from the Christian Brothers. In 2009 only five remained; none attended the Juniorate. The verse "Many are called but few are chosen" still winnowed the ranks. I can't vouch for the others but my decision to withdraw from the brothers came after much agony of thought, confusion about my identity, and the lack of emotional maturity. I framed my struggle primarily as a conflict of a one good versus another good; the religious life versus the married life. A common belief concerning religious dedication in the Catholic Church asserted that a vocation to the priesthood constituted the highest calling, followed by a vocation to the religious life, even though the profession of vows wasn't a sacrament like marriage. Shouldn't sacramental theology have placed the vocation to marriage in second place? The assertion that a vocation to the religious life trumped marriage centered on the idea that a celibate religious gave his entire life to Christ and escaped the burdens of ordinary life. This specious argument implied that doctors couldn't be wives and pilots couldn't be husbands.

Lumen Gentium, one of the major documents of Vatican II, contained few references to the religious life but these few passages solidified the assertion that a vocation to be a religious surpassed marriage. "The religious state, whose purpose is to free its members from earthly cares, more fully manifests to all believers the presence of heavenly goods already possessed here below."[27]

Often, the description of a nun's life included the phrase that her vocation constituted being "a bride of Christ" although the phrase metaphorically, in theological tradition, describes the church itself. No equivalent moniker existed for the vocation of the male religious. Many times people questioned me about the essence of the brother's vocation. I gave one answer that clarified the issue—brothers were male nuns.

Comparing marriage and the religious life, the Catholic Church's belief in the permanence of marriage overrode its belief in the permanence of vows. Divorce is still on the books but a religious can be dispensed from the contract of vows by petitioning the Pope. I know the Pope denied none of the twenty-six requests from my group.

On May 10 1970 I wrote a long letter to Brother Bertrand Leo commenting on a recent essay concerning celibacy he had sent to the brothers of the district. The basic theme of my letter accused him of neglecting the role of women in the lives of the brothers. I wrote that "One must begin to look at the life we lead and see women in it." After I wrote the letter I reread it. It sounded too accusatory—I never sent it but stuck it in my journal.

In my search for myself I turned to another passage from chapter four of the first epistle of St. John. "God is love and he who abides in love abides in God." Other than my mother and father, no person, other than Ann, ever said to me at the deepest level of my person, "I love you." Me? I told her, if you really knew me, perhaps you would reconsider. I did not have a poor self-image; I had no image. She said that if she could only know me better she would love me more. I realized that the reason she loved me was because I was lovable and I had never experienced that kind of understanding of myself.

Nevertheless, at the end of the year at Manhattan College I decided to stay a brother and Ann remained in her order. When I received my assignment to teach mathematics at Cardinal Spellman High School in the Bronx, I feared I would be lost living on the top floor of a school with a population of almost 2,000 students. I requested to be assigned to the smaller community of Holy Name School on West 92nd Street which had only a half-dozen brothers who taught at Holy Name grammar school and, I assumed, the communal life would be more intimate. I was so wrong. If I thought the communities at Queen of Peace and Bishop Bradley lacked a collegial spirit, the community at 92nd Street existed in name only. Many weekends in September and October I found myself alone in the five storey brownstone house. My room on the top floor reminded me of living in a garret in Paris. I might have died there on a Friday evening and no one would have known until Monday morning when I didn't show up for classes at Cardinal Spellman.

One morning as I ate breakfast alone in the kitchen, one of the brothers who taught in the grammar school of Holy Name parish, rushed in and opened the refrigerator. I thought he might have sat down with me and had breakfast together but he apologized for his lateness. His breakfast consisted of a doughnut and a bottle of beer as he hurried out the door.

I had no one to talk to. When Ann called late at night I stretched the phone cord into my room from the corridor, sat down on the floor, crossed my legs and talked to her for hours.

During the last month at Manhattan College on July 27, 1970 I wrote a question in my journal. "Can we live [the religious life] and still be something toward each other?" I had invested my entire youth with the Christian Brothers and she believed I had not the courage to leave. I vacillated, wavered and hesitated to make any decision. I had decided; hadn't I? Ann was correct but the courage would come. I wrote the next entry in my journal almost three months later on October 14, 1970. "Since I last wrote, almost three months ago, I think I have undergone some tremendous changes. I am getting nearer to some very serious decisions." Two day later I wrote, "I think I'll jot off a little note to Ann in her new home to show her I am thinking of her and wishing the best for her." But in early November my emotional tide turned and I wrote that "I have a strong feeling that I shall rarely see Ann again."

In the Scholasticate in Washington two members of the faculty studied for their doctorate in clinical psychology. Several times during those years I spoke with them about some problem. I called Brother Paul, now on the faculty at Manhattan College, and asked if I could meet with him. I felt I had to speak with a professional to convince myself I wasn't going mad with anxiety. The entries in my journal from September 1970 to January 1971 reveal a person whose emotional life resembles a yo-yo with perpetual energy and in my weekly conversations with him I started to clarify my own reflections.

On November 28, I wrote in my journal that I spoke with another brother. I met him in his room on the first floor of the Holy Name

Community as he packed his bags. He told me he had met a woman about six months ago and was getting married shortly. "What speed," I wrote. "Am I too slow or do these people perceive the problems and the solutions faster than I."

I realized one reason for my sluggishness centered on the conclusion that, if I left the brothers, the previous fifteen years of my life might have been wasted. But, if I remained, would I be throwing the remainder of my life away just to save the beginning. Understanding my past and accepting it became a concern.

On January 8, 1971 I wrote about my relationship with Ann, "It's over." On January 10 I noted that I hadn't seen her in three weeks and the relationship "seems dead." It is always darkest before the dawn.

On January 27 I wrote Ann a letter and said "I miss you very much…and find it very hard to be without you." On January 28 I wrote in my journal, "I have decided."

On Friday evening January 29 I stayed up past midnight and read and meditated on the first chapter of *On Becoming a Person* by Carl Rogers. I liked the title; I thought it referred to the exact events of my life. Rogers wrote, "I have found that it does not help, in the long run, to act as though I were something I am not."[28] Simply translated I took it to mean "Was I really meant to be a brother?"

Rogers continued, "I have found it highly rewarding when I can accept another person." Another simple translation for me—should I accept Ann into my life? I whittled away at secondary issues and the core point emerged alone—did I want to commit myself entirely to one person?

Back in 1964 when Brother Augustine told me about the death of my father I asked him if three of my friends might attend the funeral. He honored my request and of these three persons, all of whom withdrew from the brothers, I am still friends with two of them. The third, after he left the order, disappeared like the morning dew, evaporated in an instant. I assumed he was gay—I had heard as much—and some years later rumors circulated that he died of AIDS. I was quite sad. Many years before in the Novitiate Brother Benilde picked us to be cantors for the singing of Vespers and Compline on holy days and we spent many moments practicing.

If he thought that his sexual orientation excluded me from being his friend, I would have told him it did not. Several of my friends are homosexual but they might better be described as acquaintances. I see them irregularly and our relationship is hardly profound. In the Christian Brothers, as far I knew, several brothers espoused homosexuality but they represented a minority. Most of the brothers I encountered lived heterosexual lives. In either case, a community of religious precluded the total commitment of one person to another. I had friends, good friends in the brothers, who gave me advice when I asked (and sometimes when I didn't) but friendship had its limitations.

That night, the more I read *On Becoming a Person,* the more my decision formed like a Polaroid photo coming into focus. At the end of the first chapter Rogers concluded that "Life, at its best, is a flowing, changing process in which nothing is fixed." One of the stock phrases of the religious life urged us "to strive for perfection." I remember a quotation attributed to Cardinal Newman that "to live is to change and to be perfect is to have changed often." I closed Rogers's book and went to sleep a little bit after two in morning.

Saturday January 30, 1971 started cold and got colder but I hardly felt any of it. I called Ann and asked her to meet me at the corner of Fifth Avenue and 84th Street just north of the Metropolitan Museum of Art where a walkway led into Central Park. I had something to tell her but I must do it in person. She was already there when I got off the cross-town bus. I arrived empty-handed; I had no ring, no flowers nor had I written any romantic poetry. I asked her to marry me and she accepted immediately. It was all over; it was just beginning. The next to last entry in my journal is on the next day. I wrote, "I should like to look at Ann anew each day of my life." She became my lover, my wife, but mostly my best friend. With one best friend I didn't need any others.

We walked around Central Park and I fished around in my pockets; I had enough money for lunch. We took the D train to Greenwich Village and ate hamburgers in a restaurant called Shakespeare's. We agreed that at least for that day we would not discuss any of the myriad details of the future: where would we live and work, when we would tell our superiors and our families. We spent the entire day rejoicing. One of the themes at our wedding is the verse from

Psalm 118. "This is the day the Lord has made. Let us be glad and rejoice in it." And we did.

We lingered at lunch and late in the afternoon boarded the D train again and rode it to the last station, Coney Island, and walked the boardwalk. I could hear the surf crash off in the darkness. The only people on the deserted beach huddled around a campfire in front of their homes—discarded cardboard boxes originally used to deliver refrigerators and washing machines. I can still see their faces, staring at us and wondering what we were doing there and why we looked so happy. I wondered what they were doing there. I took a vow of poverty but these people were the poor.

The last entry in the journal is five years later. I wrote, "Where has the time gone? Into living and loving."

ॐॐ

Most brothers who withdrew from the order did so quietly and without explanation. I did not; I wanted people to know how I suffered. In a letter dated May 10, 1971 I wrote an open letter to the Brothers of the Christian Schools. In it I stated my belief that I, and many others, had a temporary vocation. I also stated that the Brothers of the Christian Schools in 1971 were not the same institution I joined in 1956 as a sophomore at Barrytown. I had a conversation once with a brother who said that he did not withdraw from the brothers but that the brothers had withdrawn from him. He may have been right.

Why did all this happen not only to me but so many others? There are, literally, hundreds of thousands of similar stories. Some observers of this historical era maintain the Second Vatican Council caused all the consternation for the church in general and religious in particular. I disagree; it was only a catalyst. It would have happened anyway. The idea of withdrawing popped up in my mind as early as the first few months in the Novitiate and steeped stronger prior to my profession of final vows. Deep down I knew I would live the second half of my life differently that the first.

As for people leaving the religious life, others travelled that path before I did and shared their turmoil. In 1956, a book by Kathryn Hulme explored this question in her book *The Nun's Story*. Gabrielle Van der Mal (Sister Luke) concluded that she could serve God just as well as a nurse outside of her religious order.

Some not only leave their religious order or the priesthood but leave the church as well. Charles Davis, a British priest and theologian, wrote in his book *A Question of Conscience*, "On 4 December 1966 I decided to leave the Roman Catholic Church." I can well understand his radical decision but I stayed. Roman Catholicism appears to be a gene I have.

One thing I did realize; I still had a noble vocation—to be a teacher.

Acknowledgements

Most books have one author but many architects.

I am indebted to my many writer friends, , who read and commented on the entire manuscript faithfully, and especially Carol Barkin, eminent editor, whose suggestions and ideas were invaluable.

I am humbled by my association with all the members of the Brothers of the Christian Schools. Their wisdom as teachers shaped my life for which I am forever grateful.

Ann, my wife and best friend, knows the essence and heart of this memoir can be summarized in one sentence: the core will always be there.

Notes

1"Recalling Careers That Struggled to Advance 2 Blocks at a Time," Sewall Chan, The New York Times, August 1, 2005.

2The Riverdale Press, *Enrollment Still Climbing at Area's Largest School,* June 23, 1955, page 14.

3Text of the Profession of Perpetual Vows by the Brothers of the Christian Schools. The word gratuitously in the profession of vows originally meant "free of charge," that is, the students paid no fees.

4*A Concise History of the New York District.* Brother Luke Salm, F.S.C. Unpublished.

5Rule and Foundational Documents. John Baptist de LaSalle. Translated and edited by Augustine Loes, FSC and Ronald Isetti. Lasallian Publications, Christian Brothers Conference, Landover, Maryland. 2002.

6This was probably either a show from the

Omnibus TV Series that originally ran on the Hallmark Hall of Fame show in 1953 and was rebroadcast some years later or on the ABC Network in 1956 or 1957 or perhaps a production of the "DuPont Show of the Month."

[7]*Notable Speeches in Presidential Campaigns* , Robert F. Friedenberg. Page 49. Greenwood Publishing Group, 2002

[8]*The Committed: A Sociological Study of the Brothers of the Christian Schools*. William Ammentorp. Saint Mary's College Press, Winona, Minnesota. 1968.

[9]*On Not Leaving It to the Snake*, Harvey Cox. Page viii. Macmillan, 1967

[10]The Christian Brothers in the United States 1848-1948: A Century of Catholic Education. Brother Angelus Gabriel, F.S.C., Ph.D. The Declan X. McMullen Company, Inc. New York. Page 260.

[11]A Man For All Seasons, Robert Bolt. Page 4. Bellhaven House, Scarborough, Ontario, Canada. 1960

[12]*The Christian Brothers in the United States*,

Declan X. McMullen Company, Inc, page 324.

[13]The Christian Brother in the United States. Brother Angelus Gabriel. The Declan X. McMullen Company, Inc. 1948. Page 260.

[14]I, John Baptist De La Salle, Brother Leo Kirby, FSC. St. Mary's Press, Winona, Minnesota. Page 20.

[15]An Actor Prepares. Constantin Stanislavski, New York; Theater Arts, Inc. 1945. Page 73.

[16]*A Concise History of the New York District.* Brother Luke Salm, F.S.C. Undated.

[17]*An Actor Prepares.* Constantin Stanislavski. New York: Theatre Arts, Inc. Page 73.

[18]Conjectures of a Guilty Bystander. Thomas Merton. Image Books, 1968. Introduction.

[19]An Actor Prepares. Page 86.

[20]An Actor Prepares. Page 86.

[21]The Catholic Worker, March/April 1967. Pages 2,7,8.

[22]Out of the Cloister, Helen Rose Fuchs Ebaugh, University of Texas Press, 1977. Page 68.

[23]The Committed. William Ammentorp. Saint Mary's College Press, Winona, Minnesota.

[24]Ibid. Page 191.

[25]Women in the Vanishing Cloister. Helen Rose Fuchs Ebaugh. Rutgers University Press. Page 47.

[26]Out of the Cloister, Helen Rose Fuchs Ebaugh, University of Texas Press, 1977. Page 68.

[27]Lumen Gentium, chapter 6, number 44.

[28]*On Becoming a Person.* Carl Rogers. Houghton Mifflin Company, page 16.